A
GENERATION
OF
ALIENS

JOHN HARMER

A GENERATION OF ALIENS

By JOHN L. HARMER

Edited by Cheri A. Loveless

Published in the United States of America

ISBN: 978 – 0 – 9791756-0-2

51995

THIS BOOK IS DEDICATED TO

DR. WILFORD DEAN BELNAP, M.D.

Who as a practitioner of the healer's art is

also one of the "noble and great ones."

And to the honored memory of

DR. VICTOR BAILEY CLINE, Ph.D

(1925 – 2013)

Who as a psychologist and a brilliant

academician was a courageous pioneer

in identifying pornography as an addiction

FORWARD

As my wife and I sat in a favorite restaurant waiting to be served, we watched a young family select the table next to us.

Both parents approached the table talking on their cell phones. As soon as the teenage daughter was seated, she took out her phone and began texting; the next sibling, a boy of about twelve, followed suit. The youngest, a boy apparently eight or nine years of age, was the only one who took time to look at the restaurant menu for a moment; then he proceeded to kill monsters on an electronic device.

After the frustrated waitress finally got the family to give her their orders, they all returned to the electronic media that governed their lives. Only when the food came did anyone speak. It was the younger boy, who described in great detail how many "aliens" he had killed.

The word *alien* has remained with me since that moment.

al•ien

different in nature or character

(Webster's Seventh New Collegiate Dictionary)

My wife and I are the parents of ten children. We feel we raised them in a true "golden age." I remember watching their grandmother, my mother, entertain them with stories of her childhood. She remembered vividly when electricity came to her home, the first time she saw an automobile, the first time an airplane flew over their town, the first time she saw a motion picture. When one of our children asked her what was the most impressive miracle she had seen in her life, she responded, "... running water in the house."

Today, four of our children are successful attorneys; two are highly placed business leaders; one is a retired Navy Commander, another an opera star, still another a nurse practitioner; and the last has a Master's degree in music education. Our lifetime has been filled with graduation ceremonies, weddings, and the births of grandchildren. We enjoy literally thousands of photographs of joyous memories.

We should have dreams of even greater happiness for our grandchildren than we had for our children. But instead of feeling a confident anticipation for their future, we are filled with foreboding. The upcoming generation is experiencing the extreme sexualization of daily life without any understanding of how this is changing the world they will soon inherit.

According to a clinical psychologist specializing in teenage sexual addiction:

> "Boys don't talk about sex anymore. They sit there in silence, staring at hardcore pornography on their cell phones, swapping images of astonishing sexual violence as if they were Pokemon cards . . .
>
> The average child sees their first porn by the age of just 11. Between 60 and 90 percent of under-16s have viewed hardcore online pornography, and the single largest group of internet porn consumers is reported to be children aged 12 to 17 . . . the first generation to grow up seeing rape and sexual violence as a societal norm . . .
>
> . . . [R]esearchers in Sweden found that only limited exposure to porn changed boys attitudes towards their girlfriends – they found "normal" sex boring, and wanted

to experiment more . . . [W]hat kind of intimate relationships will our children be capable of forming when they mature into adults?"

The answer to his question, if current theories in psychology are correct, is that they will not be able to form any intimate relationships.

A surprising percentage of teens who seek out pornography will become addicted to it. This addiction will cause them to become increasingly alienated from day-to-day life until, as adults, they will eventually lose their jobs, their sense of normalcy, and their families.

A smaller but more frightening percentage of those addicts will attempt to act out scenes from the increasingly violent pornography they ingest – such as gunning down a motion picture audience or children in a classroom like an alien attacking earthlings.

This book is the testimony of an old warrior who has spent fifty years in the trenches battling the production and distribution of obscenity – as an attorney, as an elected public official, and as a citizen activist. It is my last warning: We must win the war against pornography.

This book summarizes my perception of how the United States has become a society so saturated with the profane and the vulgar that soon the rising generation may lack any ability to choose between good and evil, right and wrong, decency and debauchery.

It describes how my generation initiated the end of a golden era, the end of childhood for the rising generation and, quite possibly, the end of the American Republic.

I write it with the hope that someone, or maybe many "someones," will pick up the torch and lead others to stop the filth that creates the aliens who threaten to destroy us.

Introduction

THE MAKING OF AN ALIEN GENERATION

I have written this book to warn those who are morally concerned about the sexualization of society that the upcoming generation is not simply choosing a more "liberal" lifestyle. It is being "alienated" from basic values and commitments that previous generations of Americans have taken for granted for centuries.

During the past half century, the American culture has become so desensitized to that which is disgusting and indecent that the rising generation has no way of avoiding continuous exposure to obscenity. Worse, they have no way of understanding how decadent our society has become compared to what it was less than a generation ago. They simply assume that this is the way things are supposed to be.

The data regarding teenage venereal disease and abortions performed on teenage unwed mothers, the tragic increase in the sexual abuse of children, and the breakup of families are so commonplace that there is no longer a general awareness or understanding of what constitutes a morally upright society.

Today we alienate our children from childhood through television programs that exhibit couples engaged in sexual intercourse. This is not "pay per view" television, but television on network channels. Ocular science has determined that it takes only three tenths of one second for an image to pass through the eye and be indelibly planted in the brain – enough time for previously innocent children to have those sexually explicit images implanted in their minds thirty or forty times in less than one minute.

Most people who are now grandparents remember being sent to school with the simple parental admonition, "Be home before dark." Now any parent who can, drives their children to school or to the bus stop and is there to meet them as soon as school is over. If a child must walk any distance, he or she is strictly instructed to "never take a ride with anyone you do not know!" In other words, our society is so full of predatory deviants that our children are no longer safe on the streets of their own neighborhoods in bright daylight.

Today's grandparents also remember when Christmas carols were sung by the school choir, when graduation ceremonies began with prayer, when Abraham Lincoln's initial Thanksgiving proclamation was read over the school loud speaker in which Lincoln admonished the people of America to "fast and pray for forgiveness." History teachers taught about Washington's farewell address and his admonition to "never forget that our freedom came about because of divine providence."

In those days, most of the sexual slang terms now commonly heard on grade school playgrounds weren't learned until long after high school. Divorce was a matter of shame, and motion pictures did not need a rating system because they were all suitable for family members of every age. Courtesy, civility, and men standing up in the presence of a woman were simply part of our everyday culture. Concepts like road rage or date rape as societal phenomena weren't even a thought. Hard rock lyrics where "daddy" describes beating "mommy" to death with his bare hands and then throwing her body into the river were still two generations away.

Many dismiss such "nostalgia" as evidence of a simple agrarian mentality far removed from the supposed realities of the world in which we live. With a shrug of the shoulders, they smugly dismiss the idea that those times reflected a more civilized, dignified, and refined society. They choose to ignore the statistical evidence of the horrific price we now pay in terms of human suffering, family dissolution, and the financial burden of medical costs and law enforcement now carried by society as a whole.

How did this harvest come to pass?

In the biblical parable of the wheat and the tares, a weed that resembled wheat was allowed to grow with the wheat until the difference between the two could be established. When a huge number of tares (the weed) were finally discerned, the servants asked the Master, "Who did sew tares among the wheat?" The Master answered, "An enemy hath done this."

I'm reminded of one of the most famous messages in American military history, sent by Captain Oliver Hazard Perry during the War of 1812. The message simply read: *"We have met the enemy and they are ours."* In 1968, Walt Kelly, the cartoon humorist for the comic strip "Pogo" modified Perry's message to say: *"We have met the enemy and they are us."*

As our society struggles for moral survival amidst the backwash of teenage suicide, drug abuse, sexually transmitted diseases, pornography addiction, homosexual and lesbian seduction, and the alarming dissolution of families, we ponder (as did the servants observing the tares), *"Who is the enemy that has done this?"* I suggest the answer may well be, *"We have met the enemy, and they are US!"*

My generation allowed it to happen before our very eyes. As the enemy was sowing the tares of contempt and mockery for the traditional family and the attributes of decency and virtue, we who had been called "the greatest generation" failed to recognize that the seeds being sown were full of poison.

In the history of mankind, each generation leaves a legacy of some kind – even if only a legacy of having done nothing worthy of note. Assuming a generation begins and ends with events that unfold within a period of about seventy years, I am part of a generation that began in 1940 with the onset of World War II. What is my generation's legacy?

Many will recite as our legacy the so-called advances in science, medicine, industrial production, and technology and will measure the "quality of life" by the presence or absence of the various trappings that surround their physical persons. However, I wish to comment on "the quality of life" as measured by what has happened *within* us as opposed to what has happened *around* us.

The generation that preceded my own – a generation that spanned from the end of the American Civil War through the Great Depression – had ample opportunity for abandoning a legacy of inherited values like morality, integrity, and dignity. They grew up in the aftermath of a civil war that took over half a million lives. They endured the societal strains of World War I, the "roaring twenties," and the economic collapse of the 1930's that plunged half of the nation's population into near or total poverty.

Yet, with so many excuses to justify turning away from traditional virtues, just the reverse took place. They not only overcame devastating circumstances, but emerged from them stronger and more worthy of emulation than those whose legacy they inherited.

My generation inherited those virtues by which our fathers won the greatest military conflict of all time, rebuilt a Europe that had been devastated with human suffering and carnage heretofore unknown, and initiated a time of material abundance and prosperity for the majority of Americans never before available to any but the most wealthy.

So who planted the tares of pornography, drug abuse, and teenage pregnancy that have now grown up in the midst of the wheat? Who decided that the answer to rampant sexual diseases among teenagers was the mandatory distribution of condoms? Who decided to have eleven- and twelve-year-old students take health "education" classes where cucumbers are used to demonstrate how to use a condom? Who facilitated the concept that abortion on demand should be paid for by the state and given to teenagers without requiring parental consent?

We did! We did it by our silent assent and our failure to act. And the result of our indolent and passive response to the challenge was to create a generation alien to the attributes of dignity and morality, a generation with no background in the kind of thinking that produced those community standards that virtually everyone embraced not long ago.

That alienation is going to have enormous consequences for the future. In fact, how the alienation of the next generation is handled will impact the very nature of our society. It may well decide whether the future will change our culture into another Gomorrah or an ennobled extension of our original heritage.

Chapter 1

Pornography – An Addiction that Changes Your Brain

Some people consider it prudish to write a book about combatting pornography. Perhaps they think pornography is only about sex. It's not. Pornography is ultimately about violence.

Unfortunately, the American public at large does not comprehend this real and disturbing connection. Unless you have firsthand experience with a friend or a family member whose life has been taken over by pornography, or unless you have had your own struggles with it, you are unlikely to understand the following:

1. Almost everyone today is, at sometime during childhood, exposed to sexual images that disturb them. In fact, children in the upcoming generation are routinely exposed to more "hard" pornography than any proceeding generation.

2. Some youth and adults, drawn by morbid curiosity, continue to seek out additional graphic images. Viewing pornography regularly can become an addiction every bit as forceful and frightening as an addiction to hard drugs.

3. Addictions create observable physical changes in the human brain. In the case of both drugs and pornography, functional magnetic resonate imaging (fMRI) has shown that addiction creates a pathway in the brain that bypasses the center where most moral reasoning takes place.

4. Evidence is mounting that an addiction to pornography can lead to violent crime. Many criminal acts, especially against women and children, are apparent imitations of shockingly violent sexual images later discovered in possession of the perpetrators.

The four points above are steps in a cycle that begins with innocent exposure to pornographic images and ends with fascination with or involvement in violent behavior. The link between the innocent first step and the awful implications of the last step is addiction – something we hear a lot about, but likely do not understand.

How Addiction Changes the Brain

Judith was a young mother from a large immigrant family. Her grandparents had come to the U.S., taken whatever menial paid labor they could find, and worked hard so their children would have opportunities that they had never had. In turn, her parents built a successful business and all of their children, including Judith, graduated from college.

Later, Judith married and started a family, working mainly from home by producing children's music videos for a well-known children's TV show. One day her producer called her into his office to show her the results of a study of children's eye movements as they watched the show. The show's advertisers wanted the children's attention "locked on the screen," he said, and so Judith needed to change her music presentations to compete with the fast action on the increasingly violent cartoons that vied for the children's loyalty.

It was 1973. The show was Captain Kangaroo.

Instead Judith, who was worried about how television images impacted the brain, chose to pursue an advanced degree in the effects of mass media. As she put it, "If a prestigious and responsible program like *Captain*, had to speed-up its format in the days of *Leave it to Beaver*, what would happen in the decades to come? What kind of children was television fashioning and how would these altered children change our institutions of education, theology, government, law, medicine, family – mass media itself?" (Reisman, Personal Odyssey)

In 2004 Judith (now Dr. Judith Reisman) explained in testimony before the U.S. Senate Committee on Commerce, Science, and Transportation:

Thanks to the latest advances in neuroscience, we now know that pornographic visual images imprint and alter the brain, triggering an instant, involuntary, but lasting, biochemical memory trail. . . . This is true of so-called "soft-core" and "hard-core" pornography.

And once new neurochemical pathways are established, they are difficult or impossible to delete. Pornographic images also cause secretion of the body's "fight or flight" sex hormones. . . . produc[ing] . . . intense arousal states that overlap sexual lust – now with unconscious emotions of fear, shame, and/or hostility and violence. (Reisman, Testimony)

Over the years, Dr. Reisman has gathered data from various studies of the human brain that indicate that repeated viewing of pornography may create an addiction as serious as cocaine or heroine. Where scientists once believed that the human brain became fully and rigidly developed in childhood, many now believe the brain to be a "work in progress" from birth until the third decade of life, reaching its full maturity as a person approaches his or her mid-twenties.

When the human brain encounters pornography, it treats it like any disturbing image by releasing a specific mixture of chemicals produced within the body. These endogenous "drugs," intended to shield the individual in times of danger, can be misinterpreted by pornography users as a strong sexual response, leading those who seek out pornography into an addictive habit. Dr. Reisman has

17

coined the term "erototoxins" to identify this powerful "cocktail" of internally-produced chemicals that she believes is the basis for a viewer's addiction to pornography.

The concept of a pornography addiction that is created by the brain's release of chemicals when confronted with shocking images is shared by others. Dr. Donald L. Hilton, Jr., MD, an internationally recognized neurosurgeon and student of the structure and function of the human brain, believes that pornography cannot be accurately understood until people quit assuming that those who participate in it simply have "a moral weakness, or a behavioral defect." Instead, he says, it is vital to understand "the physical basis of pornography addiction."

Beginning with studies published in the early 1990s, scientists have shown that addictions, including the so-called "natural" addictions like obesity, sex, and gambling, cause measurable changes in the brain. Dr. Hilton states:

> *All addictions appear to cause physical changes (shrinkage) in control and pleasure areas of the brain; this has been well demonstrated in both drug addictions (cocaine and methamphetamine), and in "natural" addictions . . . (Hilton, 2009, p. 52)*

In a 2009 speech before the annual meeting of the Lighted Candle Society, Dr. Hilton explained how an addiction to pornography works. He described how, in an addicted state, the process of nerve cells transmitting electrical signals becomes so overused and accelerated that, as a defense mechanism, the brain begins to "shut down or downgrade." It decreases both the production of chemicals that produce pleasure and the number of receptors that contain them. Although the body does this as an attempt to return to "normal," neurons sometimes atrophy or shrink, creating a new "normal" that has fewer pleasure-producing receptors and chemicals.

Afterwards, this reduced ability for people to create sensations of pleasure leaves them in "a state of craving." They are physically unable to return to a feeling of satisfaction without doing something to boost the appropriate chemicals back to levels that "feel good." Since they have "fewer dopamine receptors to bind the dopamine, and fewer molecules when a pleasurable experience is encountered," only a massive stimulus can make them feel what most of us would consider "good." In the case of a pornography addiction, "normal marital sexual relations with a spouse will no longer suffice, and progressively more powerful stimuli are required to satisfy an incrementally more persistent craving" (Hilton, 2009 speech).

This pathological resetting of the body's pleasure system makes it difficult to recover from an addiction. Returning to a normal way of functioning not only requires a desire to change, but a lot of time and support from others. Dr. Hilton warns, "Willpower alone will not be enough, as this is a real change in brain structure and chemistry."

Far too many professionals continue to see compulsive pornography use as a behavioral/moral issue rather than as an addiction. Producers and distributors of pornography (which makes billions in profits each year) rely on this attitude and on customers who repeatedly consume their products. Such sex industry beneficiaries have been known to recruit academics with medical backgrounds and other consultants to appear in court as expert witnesses whose testimony denies claims that pornography is addictive.

In the middle of the last century, beginning with the publication of the junk science by Dr. Alfred Kinsey, Ph.D, a secret combination of business entities came into existence to commercially exploit the fallacious assertions by Kinsey and his associates. (See chapter three of this text.) In 2007 the Lighted Candle Society published an extensive analysis of that secret combination entitled *The Sex Industrial Complex.*

Over the years the sex industrial complex gained more and more participants from the publishing industry, the financial industry, the hotel industry, and the entertainment industry. Today the world-wide sex industrial complex obtains billons of dollars each year from the sale of illicit sex. It is imperative to that secret combination that the addictive nature of pornography never be proven. Like the tobacco industry before them, the sex industrial complex resorts to any necessary means to deny the truth about the addictive nature of pornography.

Dr. Hilton and others have proven that pornography is a drug "in every sense of the word."

Pornography Is a Drug

A Wall Street executive whose mainstream company profits discretely from pornography [said]: "I'm not a weirdo or a pervert, it's not my deal. I've got kids and a family. But if I can see as an underwriter going out and making bucks on people being weird, hey, dollars are dollars. I'm not selling drugs. It's Wall Street."

Actually, pornography is a drug! In every sense of the word, as we will see, it fulfills what we, as physicians, call a drug.

Consider the drug adrenaline. Every hospital has this drug available in crash carts ready to give immediately to a dying patient whose heart has stopped..... It turns out this drug is also produced in the anticipation and acting-out phase of pornography addiction. Is it a drug only if the pharmaceutical lab makes it, and not if the brain makes the same chemical?

*What about dopamine? . . . This important drug functions as an excitatory neurotransmitter and is used in Parkinson's disease. It is obtained by prescription, made by a lab, and controlled by the FDA, as is any drug. Yet if this same chemical is made in the brain, is it not a drug just because of where it is produced? Dopamine is not only important in movement systems . . . but also important in the brain a form of **prescrip**tion drug abuse when viewed in this light.*

(Excerpt from *Pornography and The Brain- Understanding the Addiction,* from an address given by Dr. Donald L. Hilton, Jr., M.D., at the Lighted Candle Society Annual Banquet, 13 May, 2009. Used with permission.)

According to Dr. Hilton, changes in dopamine metabolism and in receptor numbers can be measured by the medical community with fMRI, PET, and SPECT scans. The frontal control and pleasure cells that "shrink in a negative feedback loop . . . can be seen structurally, using fMRI with a technique called voxel-based morphometry, or VBM."

Such imaging shows that changes to the brain caused by addiction can upset the moral decision-making area of the brain:

Studies of addicts show reduced cellular activity in the orbitofrontal cortex, a brain area we rely on to make strategic, rather than impulsive, decisions. Patients with traumatic injuries to this area of the brain display problems – aggressiveness, poor judgment of future consequences, inability to inhibit inappropriate responses – that are similar to those observed in substance abusers. (Fowler, Volkow, Kassad, and Chang, 2007)

The Need for Ever-increasing Stimuli

The similarities between the brain scans of pornography addicts and those of drug addicts is disconcerting, but it makes sense. Addiction damages the brain both physically and chemically whether it is caused by ingestion of a drug from outside of the body or by the production of a drug inside the brain itself. In either case, the addict ends up needing a more powerful experience each time he/she wants to feel "good" again.

A 2006 survey conducted in South Africa appears to confirm the need for increasing stimuli. For thirteen months, data was collected at a single place of employment from computers that some workers would use during downtime to access pornography on the internet. The computers were monitored for six "explicit factor" (EF) categories:

> EFO: normal web surfing
> EF-1: further pursuing pornographic images displayed
> accidentally
> EF-2: intentionally seeking out "soft" pornographic images
> EF-3: transitioning from soft porn to more graphically
> explicit images
> EF-4: frequently seeking out explicit "hard-core"
> pornographic images
> EF-5: intentionally viewing pornographic materials for
> which receipt and transmission were considered a
> criminal offense, such as material governed by child
> protection laws and related statutes

Four trends emerged regarding employees using computers to access pornography on the internet in the office that was under observation:

1. During the 13-month period, individuals using the office computers to access pornography gradually increased the frequency with which they visited pornographic websites.

2. Those who [eventually became "frequent users" of hard core pornographic images had begun the year in the EFO (normal web surfing) category]. The CEO of the firm conducting the survey concluded that "the urge to view sites of an explicit nature grows over time."

3. People who were frequenting pornography sites on a regular basis would do so first thing in the morning, near mid-day (usually just before the lunch break), and again at the end of the work day.

4. The days on which the office computers were used the most to access pornography were Friday (perhaps suggesting that such employees were getting a "fix" in anticipation of not viewing pornography over the weekend) and Sunday, when some employees returned to the office for a brief time just to access pornography.

Interestingly, the CEO of the firm noted that "very frequently," when employees using their computers to access pornography were warned that if they continued to do so they would lose their employment, they still continued to seek it out. This inability to use rational thought to make the choice to preserve their source of income is an indicator of addiction.

In his 2009 address to the Lighted Candle Society, Dr. Hilton compared an addict's drive to constantly seek out more pornography to something Australia encountered in their efforts to avoid chemical insecticides to control their gypsy moth population. Instead, they use insect sex attractants, called pheromones, like those naturally exuded by the female moth so the male can find her. The idea is to disrupt pre-mating communication between the sexes by permeating the atmosphere with a false insect pheromone.

Two methods are used. One is "the confusion method" where an airplane scatters an environmentally insignificant number of small plastic pellets imbedded with the scent of the pheromone. It only takes a few pellets per acre to overpower the male's ability to find the female because he is desensitized to the natural scent of the female. According to an Australian article, "The male either becomes confused and doesn't know which direction to turn for the female, or he becomes desensitized to the lower levels of pheromones naturally given out by the female and has no incentive to mate with her" (Salleh, 2000). The other technique, "the trapping method," entices a male moth looking for a female into a trap where he instead finds a fatal substitute.

Pornography works much the same way. To explain, Dr. Hilton reviewed the roles of oxytocin and vasopressin in sexual attraction. Oxytocin is "a powerful bonding hormone in females . . . released during sexuality" that increases trust and allows lactation. Vasopressin is released in males during the sexual act and is also thought to play a bonding role with the object of the sexuality. In other words, consummated sex with a human partner who is present is likely to help the partners feel a bond towards one another. However, such a sexual experience, when associated with an addiction to pornographic images, bonds the person only to "a virtual mistress of sorts" (Hilton, 2009 speech).

Dr. Hilton concluded, "I believe pornography is a visual pheromone, a powerful brain drug that is changing sexuality even more rapidly through the cyber-acceleration of the internet. It is 'inhibiting orientation' and 'disrupting pre-mating communication between sexes' by permeating the atmosphere (and internet)."

In a statement to Congress, Dr. Jeffery Satinover of Princeton University said:

> *The pornography addict soon forgets about everything and everyone else in favor of an ever more elusive sexual jolt. He will eventually be able to find it only among other "junkies" like himself, and he will place at risk his career, his friends, his family. He will indulge his habit anywhere and everywhere, at any time. No one, no matter how highly placed, is immune. And like all other addicts, the pornography addict will lie to cover up, heedless of risk or cost to himself or to others. (Satinover, 2008)*

Effects of the Search for an Elusive "High"

This never-ending search for "an ever more elusive sexual jolt" is a drive not well understood by those who have not experienced it. Dr. Norman Doidge, an author and neurologist associated with Columbia University, describes men he was treating for other problems who would bring up a concern about how much time they spent looking at pornography. They admitted to "acquiring a taste for a kind of pornography that, to a greater or lesser degree, troubled or even disgusted [them]." He writes:

> *None of these men were fundamentally immature, socially awkward, or withdrawn from the world into a massive pornography collection that was a substitute for relationships with real women. . . . [But later they] reported increasing difficulty in being turned on by their actual partners . . . though they still considered them objectively attractive. . . . The*

changes I observed are not confined to a few people in therapy.
A social shift is occurring. (Doidge, 2007)

Recalling research at the National Institutes of Health (NIH) where rats learned to press a bar to get a shot of a drug, Dr. Doidge observed that men at their computers looking at porn "were uncannily like the rats in the cages of the NIH, pressing the bar to get a shot of dopamine or its equivalent."

Many therapists have noted this link between addictions and changes in the brain. In 2009, a Mind, Body, and Spirituality training seminar was held at Harvard University where practicing psychiatrists and academics from various universities gathered to focus on issues of addiction relating to extensive television viewing that escalates into cybersex. Psychiatrist Dean Belnap, wrote:

Since 2004, a twenty percent (20%) increase in suicide rates among teenagers has occurred, with the number increasing annually. . . . The overwhelming majority of those suicides came about because of addiction in one form or another. Universities report a two hundred fifty percent (250%) increase in student requests for mental health counseling.

He noted that all presented papers were strikingly similar in terms of the extreme negative consequences (structural and functional) of cybersex addiction, including changes within the nervous system. The cases discussed, which covered hundreds of individuals in therapy, show that initially pornography was rewarding in terms of sexual desires; however, as the addiction increased, most addicts developed a great distaste for the pornography itself. At the same time, they were unable to release themselves from pornography because of the escalating crescendo of addictive patterns.

Seminar participants also discussed how the data presented confirmed the idea of progressive acting out of deviant sexual conduct that causes people to abandon normal marital relations, including normal sexual relationships, in favor of indulging their severe addiction. This brings about an almost total loss of normal couple relationships, in or out of marriage.

The opening presenter at the seminar, Dr. Herbert Benson, indicated that with addictive disorders there is a loss of function in the prefrontal lobe of the brain as well as in the remaining portion of the frontal cortex. The inability to draw on this part of the brain leads to a diminished ability to think and concentrate as well as changes of function that include "loss of conscience."

David Delmonico, Ph.D. and Director of the Online Behavior Research and Education Center at Duquesne University in Pittsburg, expressed concern that specially trained medical providers are needed to discover those patients who need thorough screening for addictive involvement in "cybersex" activities. He noted that "cybersex" activity includes problems that evolve from viewing, creating, and participating in progressively more violent forms of pornography. He confirmed the significant increase in sexualized gaming, sex chat conversations, and sexual texting by teenagers using cell phones and other mobile devices and made reference to the way in which social networking sites also serve as venues for cybersex. He also noted the increasing problem of teenagers and even eleven-year-olds who appear to need therapy for depression when, in fact, "they are in the early stages of pornography addiction."

In the Forward of this book, I presented the definition of "alien" as found in the copy of Webster's dictionary that I have on my desk.

We are watching millions of adolescent boys consume a steady diet of sexually explicit material so graphic that they have suffered both structural and functional damage to their brains. A significant part of that damage is in the left pre-frontal cortex where values are developed as the brain matures.

Our boys are losing the ability to form meaningful and lasting bonds with a future wife.

They are becoming aliens.

Chapter Two

"I Want to See Filth"

THE LINK BETWEEN PORNOGRAPHY AND VIOLENCE

When "adult" bookstores and theaters were first opening their doors across the United States, a nationally syndicated columnist tried to determine why people patronized theaters showing pornographic films. He conducted his survey by approaching people leaving one such theater. Most patrons declined to be interviewed, covering their faces and running the other way. But one woman welcomed his questions.

When he asked whether she felt the price of the ticket was tantamount to a fraudulent misrepresentation, since the film had no believable story line or anything remotely close to quality acting, she defiantly confirmed that she had found exactly what she had expected and wanted. Her parting comment was, "I paid for filth and I want to see filth!"

Pornography *is* filthy. It tarnishes what was meant to be a sacred and cherished human experience.

But its effects do not end there. If they did, we could concentrate on regulating its distribution to children while helping adults learn to judge between lust and love. We could honor a court system that punishes the distribution of pornography while protecting "freedom of speech" by drawing the distinction between displaying the Venus de Milo at a museum and openly advertising magazines with bare-breasted women in compromising poses.

However, defining attraction to and fascination with the obscene pales next to the undeniably tragic effect of pornography on those who become involved with this filth. Addiction to pornography is followed by violence and death.

29

When people willfully expose themselves to pornography, they quickly become infected emotionally, spiritually, and even physically. As their obsession with it increases, they die as to things lovely and virtuous, as to honesty and integrity. They die as to sensitivity and gentleness. They die as to the ability to express affection as opposed to lust and passion. And, in the ultimate tragedy of pornography, some addicts literally bring physical death to others.

A Teenager's Daily Diet of Violence and Sex

In our highly visual, already sexualized society, images once considered pornographic surround our children almost from birth. Recently I received an eyewitness report of a rap concert held in one of the nation's largest mid-west cities. Some two thousand teenagers paid $60.00 each to attend. My informant had previously been to many similar events, yet even he was stunned at the depth of obscenity and vulgarity contained in the lyrics and in the screaming narrative used by the musicians. The audience enthusiastically applauded and cheered the vulgar and obscene performance, and many became so agitated by the hypnotic lights and mind-numbing beat of the music that they jumped around in the isles and stood on their seats, waving their arms and screaming.

In one night, the sum of $120,000 was spent by parents on their teenage children to have them indoctrinated with talk of violence, sex, and hatred for the cultural legacy that had created the society in which they were living.

A 2010 survey by NBC's Today Show provides an insight into how we have managed to create a generation of millions of youth so accustomed to violence. The survey, which focused on the plight of working mothers, revealed that 49% of working moms had knowingly sent a sick child to school or daycare; 44% would rather be thinner than have their child be smarter; and 30% had used work as an excuse not to come home on time to fix dinner and perform other parental chores.

What does a child do when neither parent are at home? They are being brainwashed by some electronic robot. Even in homes with two parents, millions of children in their most formative years are often left with only their cell phones, video games, the television, and the internet as major sources of character training and values. What is the dominant theme in most video games and on most TV programs? Violence and sex. What is the dominant theme in the text messages that are sent over teenage cell phones? Sex. Many of today's children live on a steady diet of pornography and desensitizing violence.

Ever since fMRI technology began to confirm that some stimuli actually change the structure and functioning of the brain, a number of researchers have focused on the connection between frequent viewing of violent video games and later violent behavior by the game player.

In 2006, a study by psychologist Bruce Bartholow and his colleagues at the University of Missouri at Columbia found that people who play violent video games showed "diminished brain responses to images of real-life violence." According to the report, "People who play a lot of violent video games didn't see [real-life images of violent scenes] as much different from neutral [non-violent] scenes." Said Dr. Bartholow, "They become desensitized." Dr. Craig Anderson, of Iowa State University, who has also studied the effects of such games, said, "These brain studies corroborate the many behavioral and cognitive studies showing that violent video games lead to increases in aggression."

In November 2011, a European study on the effect of video games on adolescent children reported that gaming may affect the brain in much the same way as addictions do. Using fMRI, researchers observed brain changes in 154 teenagers as they participated in a task that simulated anticipating and receiving a reward. Frequent gamers had greater brain activity when they were given feedback indicating they were losing. This response is similar to that seen in addicted gamblers who show increased levels of dopamine in the ventral striatum when they are losing money (Kuhn, et al., 2011).

Linking Pornography with Violence

For many years, prosecutors employed clinical psychologists (such as Dr. Victor Cline, Ph.D) and psychiatrists (Such as Dr. Dean Belnap, M.D.) who testified that an addiction to pornography could be the primary causative factor in the commission of certain criminal acts of abuse, including rape and murder. Their testimonies included statistical correlation of numerous incidents involving such behavior by known pornography addicts.

Defense attorneys often responded with testimony from other expert witnesses that no scientific evidence corroborates such conclusions. However, the development of fMRI technologies has begun to provide scientific data to confirm the conclusions that the prosecutors, expert witnesses, clinical psychologists, and psychiatrists have presented in courts for over the past twenty years.

The following is a sampling of a larger summary of studies on "Pornography's Relationship to Abnormal Sexual Behavior/Sexual Offenders," compiled by M. Douglas Reed in 1989, and prepared by the National Coalition Against Pornography.

Marshall (1983)
    Eighty-six percent of rapists admitted regular use of pornography, with 57% admitting actual imitation of pornography scenes in the commission of sex crimes.

Dolf Zillman and Jennings Bryant (1984)

Massive exposure to pornography produced persisting impressions of hypersexuality in society and prompted liberal attitudes concerning the dissemination of pornography. Most significantly, it fostered callousness toward women and trivialized rape as a criminal offense.

David A. Scott (1985)

Pornography can lead to sexual deviancy for disturbed and normal people alike; pornography is addictive and is the literature chosen by sexual deviants (paraphiliacs). Users of pornography frequently lose faith in the viability of marriage.

Abel, et al (1987)

The frequency of self-reported crimes [for the non-incarcerated sex offenders studied] was vastly greater than the number of crimes for which they had been arrested.

The ratio of arrest to commission of the more violent crimes such as rape and child molestation was approximately 1:30. In terms of the less aggressive crimes . . . only 1 in 150 deviant sexual episodes actually led to arrest.

Dietz and Sears (1988)

The content of pornography to which cohorts of boys – or boys as a group are repeatedly exposed, at least during the critical developmental period around puberty – shapes the distribution of sexual deviations that the cohort or group will manifest as its members reach adulthood. . . . Obscene materials play a role in creating new and enduring unhealthy and unwholesome – i.e., prurient – interests.

Victor Cline, Ph.D. (clinical psychologist)

A common pattern of progression with many pornography users (sex offenders) is identified as:

(1) addiction to hard core pornography;

(2) escalation in the need for more shocking material;

(3) desensitization toward initially shocking material; and

(4) an increased tendency to "act out" sexual activities seen in pornography.

Perhaps the most compelling evidence of the causal relationship between pornography and violent sexual abuse of women and children comes from the law enforcement officers who so often find that the perpetrators of these crimes are pornography addicts. It appears, however, that the majority of crimes of rape, child abuse, and physical torture associated with unlawful sexual behavior, are never reported.

The victims, for a variety of reasons, usually prefer to be spared the further emotional trauma and agony of reliving the event. This includes wives and children of men addicted to pornography, who are subjected to vile abuse from their husbands and fathers. The "aliens" who have abused them are allowed to remain free of any accountability for their crimes, often because the victims have no faith that justice will be done.

Sex Industry Denials and Ted Bundy

During the mid-1990s, ample evidence was found to prove that the tobacco industry had known for years about the addictive and cancer-causing attributes of nicotine. Some cigarette manufacturers were shown to have actually added stronger addictive substances to the tobacco in their cigarettes in order to intensify the dependency of the smoker upon the tobacco. For decades the tobacco industry contended against such claims, producing myriad "scientific" reports created by highly credentialed medical doctors. The blatancy of this duplicity finally brought about some modest demands for punishment of the tobacco industry.

Equally duplicitous and deceitful have been the continued assertions by those with a financial interest in the pornography industry and their allies. The Motion Picture Producers Association of America (MPAA), the American Civil Liberties Union (ACLU), and certain magazine publishers that produce pornography claim that no direct evidence proves that pornography has any causal relationship to antisocial behavior.

In 1973, the United States Supreme Court leaned on their statements (Paris Adult Theater vs. SLAYTON (413 U.S. 49)) and wrote "...there is no conclusive proof of a connection between antisocial behavior and obscene material..." The rationale necessary to believe such a claim accepts that television advertising sells products, but denies that television programs have any effect upon the minds of the viewers – an obvious contortion of the truth.

In 1982, the National Institute of Mental Health (NIMH), after an extensive review of the scientific evidence regarding television's effects upon the viewer, issued a report with this concluding statement: "...there is overwhelming evidence of a causal relationship between violence on television and later aggressive behavior." However, the opposite argument continues to be made by the defenders of pornography today, even in the face of much clinical data to the contrary, such that testimonies of parents of children who have been raped, tortured, and in many cases murdered by individuals addicted to pornography, have been deemed "unreliable."

Apologists for the pornographers also talk about "victimless crimes," as though such a thing exists. The graphic, sexually explicit scenes combined with violence that are exhibited on the internet, television, and motion picture screens all have one message: pornography is harmless entertainment. Well-known liberal columnist, Nicholas van Hoffman, wrote:

Why is it that liberals, who believe "role models" in third grade readers are of decisive influence on behavior when it concerns racism or male chauvinist piggery, laugh at the assertion that pornography may also teach rape? Every textbook in every public school system in the nation has been overhauled in the last twenty years because it was thought that the blond, blue-eyed urban children once depicted therein taught little people a socially dangerous ethnocentrism.

If textbooks, those vapid and insipid instruments of such slight influence, can have had such sweeping effect, what are we to surmise about the effects on the impressionably young of an R or X-rated movie, in wide-screen technicolor, with Dolby sound and every device of cinematic realism?

Network television executives who deny the likelihood their programs can alter human behavior lie, and they know it. All you have to do is listen to what these same gentlemen say to their advertisers. They boast, they brag, they bellow about what an effective sales medium their networks are . . . how good they are at getting people to alter their behavior and part with their money. (van Hoffman, 1979)

Since 1995, with the emergence of fMRI, many studies of the brain have reported the correlation of pornography use and antisocial deviant behavior. From these studies, two themes have emerged: first, that an appetite for pornography soon becomes an addiction dependent upon access to pornography that is increasingly more deviant, more vile, more violent, more abusive, and more degenerate; and second, that as the assimilation of pornography continues, the desensitization of the individual to presentations of acts that would ordinarily be totally abhorrent becomes so pronounced that every normal inhibition against deviant behavior ultimately disappears.

Thus, there are known instances where pornography-addicted individuals committed crimes of such a hideous nature that many refuse to believe that one human being could or would actually do such things to another human being.

One such case is the highly publicized confession of serial rapist and killer Ted Bundy, who in the hour before his execution admitted that he began his spree of depravation and death after becoming addicted to pornography in his teenage years. Before he was finally caught he had abducted, tortured, raped, and murdered nearly thirty women. According to a transcript of his interview with James Dobson:

> *Ted: I'm no social scientist, and I don't pretend to believe what John Q. Citizen thinks about this, but I've lived in prison for a long time now, and I've met a lot of men who were motivated to commit violence. Without exception, every one of them was deeply involved in pornography – deeply consumed by the addiction. The F.B.I.'s own study on serial homicide shows that the most common interest among serial killers is pornography. It's true. . . .*
>
> *I hope that those who I have caused so much grief, even if they don't believe my expression of sorrow, will believe what I'm saying now; there are those loose in their towns and communities, like me, whose dangerous impulses are being fueled, day in and day out, by violence in the media in its various forms – particularly sexualized violence. . . . Some of the violence in the movies that come into homes today is stuff they wouldn't show in X-rated adult theatres 30 years ago. (Dobson, 1989)*

The Portrayal of Women in Pornographic Material

Another example of this progression towards violence has to do with the portrayal of women and can be seen in the results of a thirty-year study of the content of *Playboy* magazine, the best known of so-called "soft-core" pornographic publications. Quoting from a study prepared for the Ontario Human Rights Commission:

> *In Making Violence Sexy: Feminist Views on Pornography, (1993, ed. D. Russell) feminist theoreticians, Andrea Dworkin and Catherine MacKinnon, describe the discriminatory role of Playboy in establishing a stressful threatening environment for women as "less than human," as legitimate "bunny" prey to be hunted. The authors note that: "Playboy, in both text and pictures, promotes rape . . . and child sexual abuse . . . (making) a specialty of targeting women for sexual harassment: working women, including nurses, police, and military personnel; and presumptively educated women, including university students and lawyers. . . . The women in Playboy are presented in postures of submission . . . as sexual objects and commodities." (Reisman, 1993, p.79)*

Some fourteen years earlier, Dr. Reo Christenson wrote an insightful and indicting summary of another one of the widely distributed pornographic slick magazines:

> *Its message is that sex is divorced from love, commitment, morality and responsibility; that it is a purely animal act, no more and no less; that it is unrelated to privacy; that deviant sex is the most adventurous and exciting sex; that women's importance is to be found in their genital organs which are fair game for whoever wishes to exploit them; that irresponsible sex has no consequences—no venereal disease, unwanted pregnancies, abortions, premature marriages, psychic traumas. Some message. (Christenson, 1979)*

Surprisingly, the feminist movement managed for years to ignore the issue of pornography entirely. I personally and repeatedly challenged feminist leaders who appeared with me on radio and TV talk shows to explain why their zeal in promoting women's

38

rights did not deal with the most anti-feminine of all activities: pornography.

Eventually, Gloria Steinem, one of the movement's most vocal feminist leaders for nearly three decades, wrote an article attempting to "distinguish pornography from erotica." Steinem declared the depiction of "mutually pleasurable sexual expression between people who have enough power to be there by positive choice" constitutes "erotica" while any erotic message that features "violence, dominance, and conquest" is pornography. For erotica to be "erotica," she insisted, portrayals of sex may involve neither a conqueror nor a victim. She was vehement in her rejection of any pornographic attempt to convince others that, to women, "pain and humiliation . . . are really the same as pleasure" (Lederer, 1980).

Drs. Dolf Zillman and Jennings Bryant, the latter then professor of Communications and department head at the University of Evansville, reported on an extensive study of the effects of pornography upon those who consume it. They noted:

> Most men might disagree with the insinuation that in pornography all sex is rape-like and point to the apparent eagerness on the part of women to do any and everything that holds promise of yielding pleasure. Likewise, many men might take issue with the declaration of ridicule as a purpose. . . . Few would object, however, to the charge of a preponderance of the characterization of women in pornography as anonymous, panting playthings that men liberally exploit for sexual self-gratification . . .

> Indeed, pornography appears to thrive on featuring social encounters in which women are eager to accommodate any and every imaginable sexual urge of about any man in the vicinity. . . . Perhaps most importantly, and presumably a vital part of what has been referred to as "male sexual fantasy," women are portrayed as hysterically euphoric in response to just about any

sexual or pseudo-sexual stimulation they receive at the hands of the "male magicians."

Needless to say, sexual reality tends to fall short of such magic. Men, inspired by pornography, may well feel cheated and accuse perfectly sensitive women of frigidity. . . .

Russell (1980) has recently documented that women take the brunt of this type of pornography-inspired experimentation. Men, the aggressively superior gender, were found to have made women comply with their requests to try what had been seen. . . . Requests tended to be backed by brute force, and many women reported feelings of degradation and humiliation in addition to having been hurt physically." (Zillman and Bryant, 1983)

Pornography and Death

The evidence of the tie between pornography use and committing violence continues to mount, especially from clinical psychology. However, addicts who act out what they have seen are not the only concern. All viewers of sexual and sexually violent pornographic images are left with lasting impressions in the subconscious mind. These impressions influence and often warp their attitudes – about life and about other human beings. As Dr. Frederick Wertham put it:

Negative media effects do not generally consist in simple imitation. They are indirect, long range, and cumulative. Violent images are stored in the brain, and if, when, and how they are retrieved depends on many circumstances. It is a question not so much of acts as of attitudes, not of specific deeds but of personality developments. . . .

The saturation of people's minds with brutal and cruel images can have a long-range influence on their emotional life. It is an effect that involves human relations in fantasy and in fact and can become a contributing factor to emotional troubles and adjustment difficulties. . . .

With regard to sex, the explicit display of sadomasochistic scenes may have lasting effects. They may supply the first suggestions for special forms of deviancy or reinforce existing tendencies. The whole orientation of young people with regard to the dignity of women is affected. By showing cruelty with erotic overtones, we teach that there can be pleasure in inflicting pain on others. (Wertham, p. 11)

Thus, kinds of death other than physically killing human beings can result from the consumption of pornography. Perhaps most often, pornography leads to the death of a family.

When I was actively involved as a spokesman for anti-pornography efforts, after speaking to any audience – whether a group of five or an auditorium of over a thousand – I was invariably approached after the event by several people who had experienced the misery of a family destroyed by pornography. Typical of these agonizing tragedies was that of a woman in San Diego, California. After most of the audience had left, she came forward and asked to share her story. It was similar to literally hundreds I had heard before.

She and her husband had a thriving family of four children when, in some way, her husband became involved with pornographic material. His intimate behavior toward her changed from an expression of affection and love to seeking, and then demanding, participation in forms of sexual behavior totally unnatural and foreign to their marriage. When she refused to participate in his requests, he became physically violent and abusive. One day he stormed out of the home and disappeared for several days.

She later learned he had driven to Nevada and spent hundreds of dollars buying the sexual perversions that the pornography had

41

implanted into his mind. He found none of the anticipated and promised pleasures in these experiences, yet he still could not extricate himself from the emotional muck into which he had willingly wandered. The marriage ended in divorce.

Frequently I was asked by a deeply embarrassed and distraught wife if I could recommend a professional therapist who might assist her in bringing her husband back to reality insofar as their personal intimacy was concerned. Only the most intense agony of soul could lead these women to approach someone they had never before seen to plead for guidance in finding a way to restore a loved one who had become lost to them in the world of pornography.

According to my dictionary, an "alien" is a creature that is "foreign" or "unnatural." When the human brain in its most formative years is altered in its structure and in its function by the repeated viewing of sexually explicit materials, certain instincts and attributes familiar to us may be destroyed. It becomes something "alien" to those around it.

Many books have been written and films made about alien extraterrestrial creatures who want to destroy us and take over our earth. Perhaps instead we should worry about the aliens we are creating among our own culture and kin – those who will help destroy us because they will not be able or willing to participate in the preservation and the continuation of the race.

Chapter 3

HOW DID WE GET HERE? FOUR MEGA-TRENDS

In 1964, as a young attorney in Glendale, Los Angeles County, California, I engaged in my first confrontation with the producers and distributors of pornography. From then until now I have seen pornography grow from a sleazy, shameful presence found only in back alley locations into a multi-billion dollar business whose shares are traded on the stock exchanges and whose power and influence extend from the highest levels of government and academia to local kindergarten classrooms.

People often ask, "How did we get here? How did it happen?"

From my own participation in matters of public interest, I can cite four "mega-trends" that I believe contributed to a national tolerance for the vulgar in our media from our highway billboards to our most sophisticated publications. Each trend began gradually and progressed in incremental steps until they combined to produce the everyday assault that now passes for entertainment and commentary in our media.

These four trends are:

1- Mainstreaming the idea of "academic" sex research by building on the fraudulent work of Alfred Kinsey and others to replace Judeo-Christian values with revisionist philosophies in our religious and educational institutions.

2- Allowing the decline of the traditional family with its resulting loss of social capital.

3- Accepting decisions made by the United States Supreme Court that upset centuries of legal tradition based on a foundation of moral values.

4- Tolerating the emergence of the Sex Industrial Complex, a combination of powerful business and financial entities that have finally made it possible to distribute every conceivable graphic obscenity directly into every home.

In this chapter, I will briefly discuss the first two trends. The last two will require separate chapters.

Mega-Trend #1: Replacing Judeo-Christian Values with Revisionist Thinking

For centuries past, and perhaps for most of the world's history, people seem to have recognized as "good" a code of morality we think of as Biblical. Some people who considered it naïve to live by a code of behavior based on treating others as you would like to be treated seemed still to have recognized in it the ideal. Even those with no desire to abide by "rules" that required them to refrain from lying, stealing, cheating, and killing, sensed the depravity of their own actions.

However, the past century has seen a dramatic change in the religious and educational institutions of America: from an acceptance of the authority of Judeo-Christian values to a preference for certain revisionist philosophers such as William James, John Dewey, and their followers, men who saw a scientifically objective stance as the best source of truth. Throughout the 20th century, we have gradually but overwhelmingly transitioned from one to the other, until the "new" philosophies have so thoroughly permeated our institutions that many of our churches now malign, ridicule, denigrate, and reject revealed religion as a basis for human conduct.

These years of educating children and young adults to look for moral guidance only in science and reason has resulted in a prevailing philosophy among the rising generation that individuals are no longer morally responsible for their actions. A bumper sticker seen frequently on college and university campuses sums it up: "If it feels good – do it!" Thus, goodness is now defined on the basis of feeling rather than reliance upon revealed truth and centuries of experience.

Also, the presence of a growing anti-religious (especially anti-Christian) intellectual elite among the faculties of college and university campuses has had an enormous influence on the students coming through the programs on those campuses. The fruit of that influence was the erosion of moral restraints on the personal behavior of many young people who were away from home for the first time. The influence usually reserved for God and religion was abdicated to pseudo scientists for whom there were no such verities in life as "right" or "wrong."

One such academic presence was that of Alfred Kinsey.

Kinsey and the "Academic" Study of Sex

Generally, in the academic world, a strict procedure is followed to guarantee the validity of a scientific discovery before it is announced. That procedure consists of the following:

1. A research objective is defined and a protocol established according to well-recognized criteria in the scientific discipline governing the study.
2. Researchers involved in the study must not have any preconceived conclusions about its results.

3. If a research project is conducted under the auspices of a university or any other recognized research entity, it must be submitted to an Institutional Review Board (IRB) for review of the protocol and approval as a scientifically valid research objective. Without such approval, the project cannot be undertaken.
4. A reputable scientist, whose expertise in the chosen area of study qualifies him or her, is selected to oversee the project as the Principal Investigator.
5. The final report of the research findings is reviewed for its scientific credibility by an independent panel of scientists from the same discipline as the PI.
6. The final report, which also describes the protocol, is published in a recognized scientific journal.
7. The results of the research project must be capable of being replicated by other scientists who follow the same protocol.

Almost all major institutions of higher learning and independent research in the United States strive to meet these criteria. However, the University of Indiana continues to support a study carried out by a former faculty member who did not follow a single step in the criteria outlined above.

Despite well-documented evidence that this study included fraudulent and even fabricated data, the University of Indiana maintains both an academic major based on the faulty data as well as an institute named after a professor of zoology, Alfred Kinsey, the faculty member in question. The subsequent discovery of documents written by Kinsey and his associates confirm that he was obsessed with sexual perversion.

In a series of well-documented maneuvers, Kinsey was able to get himself designated as the faculty member assigned to research issues involving student sexual behavior. The way he pursued interviews outraged a number of students. In fact, student revulsion at Kinsey's approach became so strong that the Dean of Women Students refused to allow him to continue his bizarre intrusions into the lives of the female students. Still, his unusual conduct in both his personal life and in his capacity as a faculty member at the University of Indiana became increasingly flagrant.

In 1948 Kinsey persuaded a medical book publisher in Philadelphia to publish his book *Sexual Behavior in the Human Male*. Five years later, the sequel, *Sexual Behavior in the Human Female,* appeared. These books initiated a notable change in America's cultural view of what constitutes "normal" sexual habits and relationships.

In both books, data was presented as if it had been obtained, reviewed, and interpreted with scientific accuracy. However, closer examination of Kinsey's team and methods revealed many unexplained leaps. For example, Kinsey interviewed an inordinate number of sexual deviants, including convicted sex offenders and prostitutes, whose responses to questions were treated as a valid reflection of the U. S. population as a whole.

Credible scientists of the day repeatedly pointed out that the report lacked a valid scientific protocol. Kinsey later complained about these critics in a letter to a colleague: "Psychologists of Terman's generation [suggest] we confine ourselves to a good, normal, middle-class group" [ref: Reisman]. He clearly realized that the people interviewed for his database were not such a group.

Notwithstanding this and other lacks of conformity to the standards of scientific inquiry, Kinsey's books became national best sellers. One commentator of the day jokingly noted that, with the exception of the Bible, no two books in the English language were quoted more by people who had never read them!

The American mass media unabashedly promoted Kinsey's books – quoting, adulating, and essentially enshrining him as an expert a full year before his first book was released. Dr. Judith Reisman, today's foremost expert regarding Kinsey and his "science," wondered how "this bow-tied, Midwestern zoology professor become a savvy public relations wizard capable of conducting a book promotion rivaling that of a Madison Avenue ad agency" (Reisman, 1998, *Crimes & Consequences,*).

She was able to document how Kinsey and his benefactors (including the Rockefeller Foundation) set in motion a massive publicity campaign preceding the release of each volume. The racy responses of sexual deviants and acknowledged pedophiles in Kinsey's database provided headlines that easily fueled public interest. The impression from that day's glossy magazines was that Kinsey had discovered that Americans were secretly obsessed with sex and that many people led private lives filled with illicit and deviant sexual encounters.

Via publications like *Time, Life, Fortune,* and even *The Reader's Digest,* Kinsey's false data about the alleged sexual behavior of America's population reached almost every home and helped forge a new perception of an oversexed American public. The major daily newspapers of the time also presented Alfred Kinsey's conclusions as confirmed scientific data. By the time his second book appeared in 1953, the public was so consumed with his titillating details that voices of credible scientists, academics, and statisticians who were pointing out the obvious fallacies in Kinsey's work could not be heard.

In other words, a nation that had just fought and won a world war, strengthened by a motivation that came from its Judeo-Christian heritage, was led to believe that most of their fellow citizens were hypocrites who privately accepted what was then regarded as the values of the sleaziest members of society. Having been thus persuaded to discard the concept of being decent and virtuous followers of their forbearer's heritage of moral integrity, the American people became victims of a sequence of events that no one could have anticipated when that war ended in 1945.

Kinsey's Continuing Influence

Out of Kinsey's patently false findings have come curriculum programs on sex education in colleges and universities throughout the country. Graduates of these programs have filtered into the public school system, and amazingly enough, into a number of parochial school programs as well. Through the work of Siecus (Sex Information and Education Council of the United States) and Planned Parenthood, both of whom receive substantial financing from the federal government, children were introduced to the specifics of sexual intercourse that their parents had not seen or heard until the end of high school.

In the summer of 1983, more than fifty of the FBI's most experienced agents attended a meeting held at the FBI's facilities at Quantico, Virginia. These men and women were investigators of violent sex crimes, particularly crimes involving the kidnapping and murder of children. They had seen everything that the most degenerate mind of a sex fiend could make happen.

They came to hear Dr. Judith Reisman, who had received a contract from the Justice Department to do a page by page analysis of the three most widely read pornographic magazines in the United States: *Playboy, Penthouse,* and *Hustler.* With a staff of over a dozen researchers, she had documented how these three publications had produced articles and cartoons capable of creating an addiction to pedophilia through their pornographic presentations of children.

49

At first the attendees provided only polite attention. However, within minutes their minds and eyes were riveted on the screen at the front of the room as Dr. Reisman showed examples from a collection of over four thousand cartoons that had appeared in these publications over twenty years, in which children were presented as objects of sexual lust.

These hardened criminal investigators thought they had seen it all, but they were stunned by what these publications had been doing to poison the minds of millions of readers. The reality of what twenty years of sexual brainwashing had accomplished led many of the agents later to take the time to write Dr. Reisman about their feelings regarding what they had seen. Without exception, their letters expressed how surprised and sickened they were to discover how these three magazines had carried on such a long campaign of seducing men into abusing children. The innocent blood of those abused and murdered children still cries out for justice against a society that smugly allowed these magazines to continue such a campaign.

The publisher of *Playboy* used the supposed "science" of Alfred Kinsey to justify his decades-long campaign to sexualize the American public. In one magazine editorial, he wrote:

> One of the first books after the War to become a best seller because of sex was a statistical survey by Dr. Alfred C. Kinsey and his associates of Indiana University. *Sexual Behavior in the Human Male*, followed by *Sexual Behavior in the Human Female*, proved that the public earnestly wanted to know more about sex, and the sham and secrecy that had for so long surrounded the subject finally began falling away.

> "The Kinsey Report" was the first extensive scientific study of sex practices in the U.S., and it unquestionably affected

behavior even as it reported it. America's sexual hypocrisy was out in the open – we had been preaching one thing and practicing another due to the country's purityrannical zealots, who had successfully sustained the image of sex as sin by keeping it in the shadows."

According to Dr. Reisman, "Since its second issue in 1954 through the year 1980, *Playboy* magazine had systematically produced 3,004 cartoons and photographs of children as unharmed observers or victims of rape, sadism, bestiality, ritual sacrifice, homosexuality, and incest. Such sexually debased children were not accidentally included in *Playboy*. They didn't just slip in unawares. Remember, Brooke Shields' nude photos - oiled and posed seductively at age nine – were first published by the *Playboy* press" (J. Reisman, CD provided to the author.)

An "Academic" Conference on Porn

Over the years, the academic community has come to embrace the subject of pornography itself as proper classroom material. Deservedly obscure academics, who might have had no other way to distinguish themselves, promote the "study" of pornographic materials and their "effect" upon men, women, and even children. In August 1998, this curriculum of so-called higher education descended to the depths when California State University at Northridge sponsored the World Conference on Pornography.

For three days this conference presented an unending stream of hard-core pornography under the guise of "academic analysis." The conference also presented awards to the producers of hard-core pornography films, to the actors and actresses of the same, and to the various exhibitors who "pioneered" the introduction of hard-core pornography throughout the world. The organizers of the conference disingenuously stated, "While the organizers do not agree with all of the various positions that may be presented, we strongly endorse the right of presentation and discussion."

Among the most disappointing and amazing aspects of an event that could only be described as "beyond comprehension" were the number of women faculty members who actively participated, and the significant amount of pornographic material being produced by women for women. The conference left no doubt that, at least in the United States, women have become more than equal with men as they have aggressively entered into the production and distribution of pornography.

Displayed at the conference was every form of hard-core pornography that has been produced, from comic books to expensive motion pictures, from amateur home videos of excretion and sexual perversion to specialized highly professional videocassettes produced for homosexuals and lesbians.

Another award went to one of the California attorneys who made a fortune defending hard-core pornography in the courtroom. The national president of the American Civil Liberties Union (ACLU), Nadine Strossen, gave the keynote address and spoke with pride over the fact that the lawsuit that killed the Communications Decency Act – the initial attempt by Congress to restrict the transmission of pornography over the internet – bears the name *Reno v. ACLU.* (The ACLU immediately earned financial support from the MPAA and the pornography industry by filing a lawsuit against the act.)

In her book, *Defending Pornography: Free Speech, Sex and the Fight for Women's Rights,* Strossen presents all of the predictable arguments for unrestricted distribution of obscenity. She typifies the feminist hatred of the traditional family unit, especially the role of the husband and father in providing for and being responsible for the welfare of the family. In a press interview after her speech, she noted sadly that the one internet obscenity case the ACLU lost was on the issue of community standards. The court held that the phrase "community standards" need not be extended to cover the entire nation. Having a "standard of decency" that covered the entire nation would have meant reducing every community to the lowest standard in the country (possibly Los Angeles).

Almost all human beings recoil at the sight of a venomous serpent. The initial reaction to pornography is usually the same, one of disgust and revulsion at the sight of something so abhorrent. But as darkness replaces daylight, the allure of pornography grows. Unlike the venomous serpent, but very much like the boa constrictor, pornography slowly wraps its coils around each victim until escape is no longer possible. Death – always spiritual, almost always emotional, and sometimes physical – is the inevitable result.

The presumed "science" of Alfred Kinsey provided a fraudulent scientific justification for an unrestrained response to carnal appetites and passions. His fabricated research became the justification for disciples who reaped enormous financial profits by exploiting the allure of such lustful conduct. Much as Lenin and Trotsky provided the concepts of Karl Marx with presumably justifiable conduct by government, so glossy magazines advocating Kinsey's perverted ideas of human behavior became daily fare in the culture of western societies.

Megatrend #2: Decline of the Traditional Family

At about the same time as mass media adulation of Kinsey's "science" was marching into the classroom, a variety of other germs were invading the already weakened American body politic. Liberal academics and media commentators supported one another in working zealously to bring their kindred spirits into prominence.

For example, William F. Buckley's book, *God and Man at Yale*, reveals how an ultra-liberal faculty at Yale consciously distorted the teaching of history and philosophy in order to saturate the student body with an unChristianized version of the rise of the American Republic.

In 1962, the pharmaceutical industry introduced "the Pill" into the marketplace, assuring the public that its use would be restricted to "medical purposes only," as directed by a physician issuing a prescription. Hardly anyone believed this blatant hypocrisy, least of all the medical profession whom the pharmaceutical industry recruited as the gatekeepers for the protection of the public morals. Immediately upon its arrival in the local drugstores, the pill made possible sex for recreation rather than procreation for millions of young women.

Since recreational sex was a clear and direct violation of both Mosaic Law and the admonitions of St. Paul, some church attendees needed a way to reconcile their newly found views of morality. Churches began to solve this dilemma of abandoning Moses and Paul by beginning to stress activism for "social justice" as opposed to advocacy for social virtue.

For many parishioners, the worship of Jesus Christ and living by the Ten Commandments was eventually replaced with the deification of trees and animals. Thus environmentalism as a false religion swept across the country in the sixties and seventies, perhaps as a way in which an otherwise guilty conscience could still be "on the Lord's side" without the inconvenience of self-restraint and the disciplined moral behavior required of the Christian disciple.

An economic upsurge following the Korean conflict also helped make traditional morality irrelevant. The dependence upon divine providence that the Great Depression had required of millions of people who otherwise might have abandoned their hope for ultimate survival now could be forgotten. Living "the good life" made it possible for the masses to enjoy luxuries and leisure in a manner never before known among the vast majority of people. The effect of this new lifestyle on values and behavior was to make compliance with previously honored rules of personal conduct something easily set aside. Even many of those who attended church on a regular basis became much more casual in their adherence to once enshrined rules of ethical and moral behavior.

The advertising industry subtly accelerated the changing image of women from respected and revered nurturing ministers of love to the baser status of being objects for sex. Ever ready to lead out in the abandonment of traditional values, the tabloid newspapers of Britain presented on a daily basis photos of provocatively posed, scantily clad women. Their message was: these are objects of sexual gratification that one can purchase with the same thought process that drives the purchase of a pair of shoes. The American mass media eventually did even more to make woman sexual objects rather than persons.

> *When exactly did this downward cultural spiral begin, this loss of tact and refinement and understanding that some things should not be said or directly represented? When did we no longer appreciate that to dignify certain modes of behavior, manners, and ways of being with artistic representation was implicitly to glorify and promote them? There is, as Adam Smith said, a deal of ruin in a nation: and this truth applies as much to a nation's culture as to its economy (Dalrymple, 55-56).*

An American perspective on the same question comes from Dr. Robert H. Bork, in his book, *Slouching Towards Gomorrah*:

In the United States, at least, that decline and the mounting
resistance to it have produced what we now call a culture war.
It is impossible to say what the outcome will be, but for the
moment, our trajectory continues downward. This is not to
deny that much in our culture remains healthy, that many
families are intact and continue to raise children with strong
moral values. American culture is complex and resilient. But it
is also not to be denied that there are aspects of almost every
branch of our culture that are worse than ever before and that
the rot is spreading.

This downward spiral, this spreading rot is the result of the decline
of strong traditional families. Whatever the confluence of factors
that exacerbated the process, only the loss of strong families can
completely beat us down. We were assured that no-fault divorce,
increased government subsidization of families without fathers,
and sex education for grade school children would bring social
justice, psychological comfort, and economic progress to millions.
The truth is that the dollars and cents costs for law enforcement,
welfare subsidization, medical treatment of teenagers with unwed
pregnancies and adults with sexually transmitted diseases
continues to decimate real family income. More and more, the
financial burden for these failed programs falls on the shoulders of
the productive and responsible members of society through
increased taxation.

The media promulgated what turns out to have been a lie: that the
responsibility for the increase in these negative symptoms of social
decay lay with our failure to care for and properly educate the
"victims" of our unjust social institutions, that advocacy of the
"traditional two parent family" in our schools and in our laws was
responsible for creating those inequities and societal
maladjustments.

But let's take a look at what family life was like at the worst of times, in the midst of the Great Depression: twenty four percent (24%) of the men available for employment had no job; yet somehow they managed to carry on, to maintain a personal sense of dignity and sometimes even optimism. I can still remember the day in 1940 when my father finally lost the family home, and we moved from our own home "in the avenues" to one that my father rented for $1.25 a day. Our family survived because our two parents determined that what had happened to us physically would not destroy our heritage of good character within us.

Noted humorist and author Sam Levenson once described his own family circumstances in the "slums" of New York:

I was raised in a section of New York that was called a "slum" by sightseeing guides and "a depressed area" by sociologists. Both were right. Our neighborhood fulfilled all the sordid requirements with honors. We were unquestionably above average in squalid tenements, putrid poolrooms, stenchy saloons, cold flats, hot roofs, dirty streets, and flying garbage. Yet, paradoxically, I never felt depressed or deprived. My environment was miserable; I was not.

I was a most fortunate child. Ours was a home rich enough in family harmony and love to immunize eight kids against the potentially toxic effects of the environment beyond our door. Since the social scientists do not, as far as I know, have a clinical name for the fortunate possessors of this kind of emotional security, I might suggest they label them the privileged poor. Poverty never succeeded in degrading our family. We were independently poor.

Our home was a battleground in the relentless struggle not only for survival, (which even the beasts can manage) but for

survival with dignity. This was the American Revolution fourth
floor back. (Levenson, p. 12)

Social workers, after forty years of failure with high cost programs designed to rescue people like the Levenson family, will argue that this family was anything but typical of those for whom these failed programs were intended. But they were impoverished immigrants, discriminated against because of their ethnicity; the father worked twelve hours a day at a menial task and the mother remained in the home to nurture eight children. Who could have been more "typical" of the American slums at that time?

Sam Levenson explained the secret of their ultimate triumph over their environment and poverty: *"You could be a hero in your own home. Papa was. Mama was. And so was anyone who brought honor to the family."* Note the key words in that sentence: heroism, home, papa, mama, honor, and finally, family. Heroism was manifest in the daily battle; home was where the weapons for the battle, and ultimately the victory, were forged. What were those weapons? *Papa, mama,* and values such as *honor* and being one of the *family* – the nurturing empowerment of family unity.

The depression ended with the onslaught of World War II. From their family farms, from the ghettos, from the middle class sections of town, and even from the well-to-do homes up on the hill came a generation of American youth destined for greatness. In his biography of these young men and women, Tom Brokow describes them as:

> . . . *a generation of Americans that would take its place in American history with the generations that had converted the North American wilderness into the United States and infused the new nation with self-determination embodied first in the Declaration of Independence and then in the Constitution and the Bill of Rights.*

58

At the end of the twentieth century, the contributions of this generation would be in bold print in any review of this turbulent and earth-altering time. It may be historically premature to judge the greatness of a whole generation, but indisputably, there are common traits that cannot be denied. It is a generation that, by and large, made no demands of homage from those who followed and prospered economically, politically, and culturally because of its sacrifices. It is a generation of towering achievement and modest demeanor, a legacy of their formative years when they were participants in and witness to sacrifices of the highest order. They know how many of the best of their generation didn't make it to their early twenties, how many brilliant scientists, teachers, spiritual and business leaders, politicians and artists were lost in the ravages of the greatest war the world has seen. (Brokow)

These men and women were able to achieve the status of "the greatest generation" without the plethora of programs that have been thrust upon us today. They, like the Levenson family, struggled through a period of hardship in which sacrifice was the daily fare, not a once in a lifetime necessity. It was that struggle – using their own resources and their own will – that gave them strength. They did not need a band of academic elites to inform them that they were in fact downtrodden and deprived. They were the heroes of a culture modeled by attitudes such as self-reliance, honesty, and hard work.

Our Resulting Loss of Social Capital

Losing the families and homes that helped build that kind of Americans has been a loss indeed. How much has the abolition of this social heritage cost us? A monetary answer is found in what economists and other social scientists call *social capital*.

The concept of social capital was initially developed by sociologists James Coleman, Jane Jacobs, and Robert Putnam. It now figures prominently in the economic and social analyses of many researchers. Though these researchers vary somewhat in how they define it, the World Bank's 1999 definition of social capital expresses well what is at stake: *"Social Capital refers to the institutions, relationships, and norms that shape the quality and quantity of a society's social interactions . . . Social Capital is not just the sum of the institutions that underpin a society – it is the glue that holds them together."*

If the loss of our basic family institution has resulted in the toleration of pornography, the cost to our nation is enormous. It would have to include what society now has to pay for law enforcement, medical care, and increased welfare dependency as well as other costs.

According to Dr. Bryce Christensen, who has analyzed for the Howard Center what family disintegration costs our society:

Americans see a partial recognition of the dollars-and-cents effects of the crisis in social capital formation in a study released in 2008 by the New York-based Institute for American Values estimating that "family fragmentation costs U.S. taxpayers at least $112 billion each and every year, or more than $1 trillion each decade." Working from "cautious assumptions" the authors of this study emphasize that " . . . the $112 billion figure represents a lower-bound or minimum estimate of the economic impact of family disintegration." (B. Christensen)

In other words, events that began post-World War II, many of which are described within the pages of this book, have combined to eliminate trillions of dollars from the American economy. If the present trend continues, our economy will experience the same kind of erosion and ultimate exhaustion that has decimated the economies of Europe and Great Britain. This real dollar impact has taken its toll because of the subtle and incremental erosion of the one essential factor in the production of social capital – the traditional family unit.

Dr. Christensen laments the fact that the public media largely ignores this issue:

> *Again and again for the last thirty years, the message from the media about family change has been the same: Don't listen to the conservative Chicken Littles. The sky is not falling. Relax. Enjoy life. Watch T.V. This attitude looks astonishingly nonchalant to anyone familiar with the empirical evidence linking widespread family disintegration to the impoverishment of women and children, to violent crime, to mental and physical illness, to drug and alcohol abuse, to child abuse, to academic failure, and to teen suicide. But journalists do not seem to understand these linkages – or their implications. (B. Christensen, emphasis added)*

The results that we face can be ascertained from a CNN survey* carried out among entering students on our university campuses. CNN learned the following about the upcoming generation of *millennials*:

- Seven in ten millennials say sex between an unmarried man and woman is morally acceptable.
- Among millennials, young Christians are as sexually active as non-Christians.
- More than six in ten millennials support same sex marriages.
- Six in ten millennials say abortion should be legal, which is a higher percentage than is found in the general population. An even higher percentage say that abortion services should be available in local communities.

- According to a report in *The Christian Science Monitor,* three out of four say that wealthy corporations and financiers have too much power and that taxes should be raised on the very wealthy.
- Two out of three say that creationist views on evolution is outdated. (*http://www.cnn.com/2011/12/16/opinion/stepp-millennials-church/index.html?hpt=hp_bn9)

As noted by Dr. Theodore Dalrymple, it has been "the breakdown of the family structure" that has resulted in the unfulfilled promises of the liberal elite with their various programs by which the government takes over more and more family functions. It has produced the phenomenon noted by David Blankenhorn in his book, *Fatherless America,* of how government programs of subsidizing illegitimate children has foisted upon the rest of society a huge number of law breaking, welfare spending, health care consuming, non-producing individuals. As described above, the cost of nearly half a century of the social re-structuring of our society comes to over three trillion dollars in social capital.

But the cost in terms of broken homes, broken families, and broken hearts will never be measured by dollars alone.

Chapter Four
Mega-Trend # 3
HOW THE UNITED STATES SUPREME COURT
CREATED A SAFE HAVEN FOR PORNOGRAPHY

It is arguable that the American Judiciary – the Supreme Court, abetted by the lower federal courts and many state courts – is THE single most powerful force shaping our culture. (Judge Robert Bork, 1996, p. 96)

Over the last fifty years, the Supreme Court has done more to advance the presence of pornography in America than any other factor. The purpose of this chapter is to explain, from the perspective of my personal involvement in the legal fight against pornography, how this came about.

To begin, it's important to understand that judges acknowledge the existence of obscenity. They accept that the motive behind a museum's exhibition of the famed sculpture *Venus de Milo* is not the same as a magazine or motion picture presentation of a bare-breasted woman. Over the years, in judicial opinions related to issues of obscenity, the phrase "having a morbid interest in the prurient (that which excites to lust)" was often employed as a guideline for discerning the difference between art and pornography.

The difficulty in distinguishing the difference comes from the fact that, like art, pornography can be viewed as a form of expression, as Dr. Jefferey Satinover of Princeton observed in testimony before Congress:

> *It has always seemed self-evident that pornography is nothing more than a form of "expression." Its putative merits, lack thereof, or evils always therefore have been*

63

debated in terms appropriate to "expression," and our laws reflect as much. We argue over the "morality" of pornographic literature; its nature as "high" or "low" art; whether it has any "redeeming value." References to "works" of pornographic "literature" and "acts" of pornographic "dance" are enshrined at the highest levels of American constitutional jurisprudence—the words in quotation marks making it clear that the understanding of pornography as expression is foundational and unquestioned. (Satinover, 2008)

However, pornography is *not* protected by the First Amendment. Consider the following statements from the Supreme Court in cases that reference the right of the States under the Constitution to protect the moral climate in which their citizens dwell:

[T]o equate the free and robust exchange of ideas and political debate with commercial exploitation of obscene materials demeans the grand conception of the First Amendment and its high purposes in the historic struggle for freedom. The protection given speech and press was fashioned to assure the unfettered interchange of ideas for the bringing about of political and social changes desired by the people.

But the public portrayal of hard-core sexual conduct for its own sake, and for ensuring commercial gain, is a different matter. This much has been categorically settled by the Court, that obscene material is unprotected by the First Amendment. (Miller vs. California (413 U.S. 15, 1973))

This court has consistently held that obscene material is not protected by the First Amendment as a limitation on the state police power . . . The states have the power to make a morally neutral judgment that public exhibition of obscene material, or commerce in such material, has a tendency to injure the community as a whole, to endanger the public safety, or to jeopardize . . . the States' right to maintain a decent society. (Paris Adult Theatre vs. Slaton (413 U.S. 49,1973))

So how did our highest court open the door to the kind of public display of obscenity now commonly seen throughout our nation? I will tell the story as I experienced it.

Battling Porn as a Private Citizen

During the 1960s I initiated a series of lawsuits against the showing of various pornographic motion pictures. I was the plaintiff, and with my attorney, Jim Clancy, we also supplied prosecutors and citizen groups around the country with briefs and memoranda that enabled them to pursue similar litigation against such films.

Although our approach was used successfully against films in other states, the courts in California continually decided against us. I was serving as a California State Senator at the time, but I was not a law enforcement official like a city or county prosecutor. Successful lawsuits were more difficult because of this, so I began searching for an alternative legal theory – one I could use as a private citizen.

In the legal theory we eventually relied on, we used the California Penal Code provisions regarding a "Public Nuisance." For at least three centuries, the common law of both England and the United States has sustained the proposition that:

Obscene or indecent exhibitions of a nature to shock the public sense of decency are also public nuisances and indictable at common law. This label includes not only obscene and indecent theatrical performances or "side shows," but other disgusting practices. (Perkins)

Under that legal premise, citizens were able to bring cases against such "moral public nuisances" as houses of prostitution, having them permanently barred and their revenues confiscated. So we began to use the "public nuisance" provisions of California's penal code, defining on-stage live presentations of obscenity as constituting a "moral public nuisance."

In 1968, a blatantly obscene film from Sweden began to circulate in the United States. A number of states took legal action against the film and obtained judgments that it was pornographic. Their courts ordered the forfeiture and confiscation of the film.

In California the film began showing in the summer of 1969. The producers distributed a 270-page book with photographic reproductions of scenes from the film and the associated dialogue. The film was clearly pornographic, depicting in graphic detail various scenes of human sexual activity and sexual perversion.

I wrote a series of letters to the appropriate law enforcement officials protesting their lack of action in prosecuting the exhibition of the film. Finally, when it was obvious that none of the authorized and responsible officials would take action, I filed a citizen's lawsuit against the film. Although, I was an elected public official, I filed in my capacity as a private citizen.

In the ensuing lawsuit, *John Harmer vs. A Motion Picture Entitled "I Am Curious (Yellow)"* (Superior Court of the State of California for the County of Los Angeles, case number 967070), we cited the action of other states in declaring the film to be obscene. We also provided the court with excerpts from the film and from the published book. Our petition asked that the court ban the film as a "public nuisance."

Within several days of our filing of the petition in the Superior Court, law enforcement agencies suddenly awakened to the presence of the film. Throughout Los Angeles County, various city and county entities proceeded to confiscate the film and to issue citations against its exhibitors. The success of the local prosecutors in Los Angeles County deterred any further effort to exhibit the motion picture elsewhere in the state.

Later, the *Los Angeles Times* (December 31, 1969) quoted the attorney who defended the various theaters exhibiting the film as saying that our action was part of "a conspiracy" against his clients and that the action of the law enforcement agencies was "designed purely to harass" his clients from conducting their business. He also claimed that the film was protected under the guarantees of the First Amendment. The fact that the film had been found in many jurisdictions outside of California to be patently obscene was deemed of little importance.

My next effort against a pornographic production came a few months later, when a stage play opened in Los Angeles that violated several state and local statutes. It was so pathetically devoid of any legitimate dramatic or humorous content that it was difficult to understand why local prosecutors couldn't just shut it down for fraud on the basis of misrepresenting it to the buying public as a theatrical production. The so-called actors and actresses pranced their way through various scenes of nudity and simulated sexual acts.

Photos of the on-stage obscenities became pivotal as we initiated the effort to shut the production down because California's statutory prohibitions against the exhibition of obscene productions were always subject to the case law decisions of the United States Supreme Court. That is, the statutes in California made the production, exhibition, or sale of pornography illegal, but the definition of what constituted an obscene or pornographic item came from the U.S. Supreme Court.

We initially lost the *Oh Calcutta* case before the Supreme Court of the State of California in a 4-3 decision. The court at that time was dominated by liberal jurists who had no sympathy for our efforts. The outcome was approvingly summarized in the entertainment industry publication *Variety*, which noted:

> *Majority decisions in Friday's ruling said live plays in a theatre are protected under the First Amendment just as are motion pictures, magazines and newspapers. It went on to say (sic) basic purpose of the penal code section under question is to punish the crime of vagrancy – not theatrical performances.*

> *Dissenting opinion, penned by Justice Louis Burke, said the decision's effect is "to allow acts, however obscene, to be performed on the stage with complete freedom unless they are proscribed by other laws."*

The net effect of the California Supreme Court's initial decision made it difficult even for a prosecutor to successfully ban live obscene presentations on stage. However, the producers of *Oh Calcutta* then went to the city of Fresno, where we filed our lawsuit against the production based upon the "moral public nuisance" concept. The Superior Court in Fresno ruled in our favor, and the producers of *Oh Calcutta* decided they had had enough. They took their obscene production elsewhere.

However, fighting pornographic showings like these films became increasingly difficult after a string of decisions made by the

Supreme Court effectively opened the floodgates for the production and distribution of obscenity and pornography.

The Unfortunate Pornography Rulings of the U. S. Supreme Court

I have submitted briefs on cases before the United States Supreme Court regarding obscenity and pornography and have studied the decisions that the Court has handed down on this issue. I cannot and do not intend to provide a treatise on this history in a mere chapter. But I do hope to provide the average reader with a credible understanding of how the decisions of the Supreme Court, beginning with *Roth vs. The United States,(354 U.S.476, 1957)* have enhanced the legal climate throughout the United States for producers and distributors of pornography.

The Roth Case came to the Supreme Court in 1957 as an appeal from a conviction in the state of New York where Samuel Roth was an undisputed distributor of sexually morbid materials. In my view, the first and most significant error the Court made was a tactical one – that of taking jurisdiction of the Roth case in the first place. The Supreme Court could have held that obscenity is not protected by the First Amendment and, therefore, no First Amendment issue was involved if the offensive material violated the statutory definition of obscene material as enacted by the State of New York.

In other words, the Supreme Court missed an opportunity to confirm that the prosecution of obscene material is properly a local issue. Even though pornography is widely distributed in interstate commerce, the Tenth Amendment (which leaves the States and the people with all authority not delegated to the federal government) allowed for it to be handled by the state where the offence took place. Expecting the states to continue setting their own standards of decency would have made a large and important contribution to the preservation of decency and morality throughout the country.

I won't attempt to deal with all of the constitutional issues involved in the Roth case, nor the various concurring and dissenting opinions from the Court. The Court did in fact affirm that obscenity did not have any right to protection under the First Amendment. However, in a disastrous strategy decision, the Court attempted to define what constituted obscenity, creating federal involvement in the issue by establishing a "test" for what constitutes obscenity.

The definition of pornography given in the *Roth* case created a two-headed monster that local prosecutors had to deal with thereafter in order to obtain a conviction against a producer or distributor of pornography. In effect, it required the prosecutor to show that "the dominant theme of the material, taken as a whole, appeals to a prurient interest in sex" and that "the average person, applying contemporary community standards, would find that the material was patently offensive."

For the next nine years, the Roth decision would become the dominant legal test for whether material could be considered obscene. However, it allowed the pornography industry to whip the prosecution at almost every turn. The Roth phrase "taken as a whole" simply encouraged pornographers to include a known literary work in their production to avoid prosecution; the language "the average person applying contemporary community standards" revealed the naivete of the Supreme Court Justices regarding how prosecutors present a question of fact during a trial.

In 1966, the Supreme Court expanded on a phrase first used in the Roth case to add a third requirement to the prosecutor's burden. In the case of *Memoirs v. Massachusetts, (383 U.S. 413, 1966)* the Court restated the Roth criteria and then made a specific requirement that had only been suggested in Roth. Now the prosecutor's burden was to convince the judge and the jury that:

1. The dominant theme of the material taken as a whole appeals to a prurient interest in sex;
2. The material is patently offensive because it violates contemporary community standards relating to the description or representation of sexual matters; and
3. The material is "utterly" without redeeming social value.

Pornographers quickly saw in the Roth decision, and later in the Memoirs decision, that all they need do to avoid prosecution was add portions of a play by an author like Shakespeare or quote from an accepted authority on any social issue. Some began to blatantly include chapters from the Bible in their materials, and one took a report to Congress on the issue of pornography and proceeded to illustrate it with vile photographs of the most lurid and degenerate scenes of sexual perversion. Since the publication included a report to Congress from a presidentially appointed commission, it could not be "utterly without redeeming social value."

The pornography industry used these Supreme Court decisions as an open door to what became a decade of fantastic profitability. The Roth and Memoirs decisions hampered prosecutors to the degree that "adult" theaters and the "adult" bookstores were able to spread across the United States almost unimpeded. Until high tech methods of distributing pornography became even more profitable, the adult theater and adult bookstore formed the backbone of the pornographers' distribution process.

Another Burden from the Supreme Court

After Roth, a plethora of cases were brought before the Supreme Court where the producers and distributors of obscene materials skillfully argued to extend the Court's specific language in ways that had not been anticipated. This parade of cases attempting to repair the legal wreckage that the Roth decision and the many cases that followed had created finally resulted in *Miller vs. California* 1973 (413 US 15, 24-25).

The Miller decision held that:

> *The basic guidelines for the trier of fact must be: (a) whether* ***the average person, applying contemporary community standards***, *would find that the work, taken as a whole, appeals to the prurient interest ... (b) whether the work depicts or describes in a* ***patently offensive way***, *sexual conduct specifically defined by the applicable state law; and (c)* ***whether the work taken as a whole***, *lacks serious literary, artistic, political, or scientific value.*

The "Miller Test" thus has three parts, all of which a prosecutor must successfully establish in order to obtain a conviction. The phrases in bold identify the issues the Court imposed on a prosecutor to "prove": a. What is an average person? What is the community? What are the community's "contemporary standards?" b. At what point is something "patently offensive?" c. What is required to provide "serious literary, artistic, political, or scientific value?"

The effect of the Miller Test, as to what constitutes obscenity, shackled law enforcement with a hopeless task. In Miller, the Supreme Court imposed upon the few prosecutors still willing to take on the pornographers a further burden of proof that essentially made it impossible for a prosecutor to succeed in any effort to protect the community from the exhibition or distribution of obscene materials. The Miller decision was used by the Clinton and the Obama Administrations as an excuse not to prosecute pornography except in the most egregious cases of child pornography.

The second of the three tests set forth in Miller (*whether the average person, applying contemporary adult community standards, "would find that the work depicts or describes, in a patently offensive way, sexual conduct"*) led to the formation of a group of professional "expert witnesses" who are recruited by defense attorneys for the pornography industry. These individuals are primarily the progeny of the "scientific" work of Dr. Alfred Kinsey at the University of Indiana.

When a local District Attorney attempts to meet the Miller Test in order to obtain a conviction, defense attorneys generally bring in a variety of such "expert" witnesses to present evidence on the "community standards" requirement. Often these witnesses have never before been in the community where the trial is taking place; yet it can be difficult for the prosecution to effectively refute these "pseudo-sexperts" with local academics who have enough legitimate credentials.

Other Cases in California

Our local battle with distributors of pornography in California continued for another decade. In one case, the opinion of Justice Herndon effectively outlined the basis of our approach. In a strongly worded dissent, in which he sought to sustain our complaint, he summarized the content of the pornographic film *Without A Stitch* (1972):

> *The English language does not provide adjectives sufficient to describe the utter rottenness of this sordid product of sub-human depravity and greed that portrays every known form of sexual perversion. (Court of Appeals of California, Second District, Division 2, March 2, 1972)*

73

We had supplied the court with photographic evidence of the content of the film, and Justice Herndon confirmed that the film was indeed "hard-core pornography as defined in [the law and was] beyond Constitutional protection." He also noted that the exhibition of such a hard-core pornographic motion picture created a public nuisance and that our brief and allegations were "sufficient to satisfy pleading requirements."

With the facts and the law so overwhelmingly on our side, we wondered how we could lose. Yet lose we did, though never on the basis of the actual issue of whether or not the films were hard-core pornography. We lost because we were not city or county prosecutors. In other words, our complaints were civil, not criminal.

The judges always found a reason to deny our petition to close down the showing of the film. In the instance of *Without a Stitch*, the majority decided that showing the film in a closed theater to "willing paying customers" negated the public nuisance argument. Yet, as we and Judge Herndon both noted, the same legal theory had successfully closed red light district houses of prostitution, even though they were equally enclosed and frequented by equally "willing paying customers."

For several years, we continued our efforts to develop a strategy under the common law of nuisance doctrine that would allow a citizen the right to go into court and remove obscene items from his/her community. We filed two separate civil lawsuits in the Los Angeles County Superior Court in an effort to have two other pornographic films (*Deep Throat* and *The Devil in Miss Jones*) declared to be hard-core pornography and moral public nuisances so that exhibiting them in the community would be unlawful in California.

After three years of litigation, including two successive appeals to the California Supreme Court and one petition to the United States Supreme Court, two separate divisions of the California Court of Appeals handed down two conflicting decisions. In the *Deep Throat* case, one court held that only a city attorney or a district attorney could bring such an action and that a private citizen such as myself did not have standing to litigate that issue in the courtroom.

In *The Devil in Miss Jones* appeal, a second division of the same court held that it might be possible for a private citizen to allege sufficient facts to establish a cause of action, but ruled that the plaintiff would then have to start all over in the trial court and amend the pleading to attempt a correction.

In each of these cases, the courts had before them photographic time-and-motion studies that showed the irrefutable hard-core nature of the films themselves. Meanwhile, the California Supreme Court refused to rule on which of the two decisions was the correct law in the state of California.

During the course of our efforts, we did obtain one encouraging victory in the California State Supreme Court. We had persuaded the district attorney of Los Angeles County to allow us to file a petition on his behalf in the Superior Court that would recognize the authority of the district attorney to proceed in a non-criminal civil proceeding to close an adult theater as a "moral public nuisance" (*People ex rel. Busch v. Projection Room Theater, et al,* (17 Cal. 3d 42, 130 Cal. Reporter 328)).

The court ruled that a theater that regularly showed pornographic films and a bookstore that regularly sold pornographic materials "was a public nuisance which could be abated in a civil lawsuit filed by a City Attorney or a District Attorney."

This was a small first step in a process that we had been pursuing for more than six years, and which we continued to pursue elsewhere in the country with increasing success. Then the Internet appeared and made the adult theater and the adult bookstore relatively obsolete.

More Fallout from Supreme Court Decisions

In 2004, the Supreme Court heard *Lawrence vs. Texas* and held that a Texas state statute against sodomy was unconstitutional as a violation of the due process clause of the Fourteenth Amendment which protects citizens from being deprived "of life, liberty, or property without due process of law." Justice Scalia dissented as follows:

> *Most of today's opinion has no relevance to its actual holding . . .The court proceeded to apply an unheard of form of rationale [to invalidate] the Texas statute. Present state laws against bigamy, same sex marriage, adult incest, prostitution, masturbation, adultery, fornication, beastiality, and obscenity are likewise sustainable only in light of [Bowers] validation of laws based on moral choices. Every single one of those laws is now called into question by today's decision . . . what a massive disruption of the current social order [today's decision] entails. (citations omitted; emphasis added)*

Using recent decisions of the Supreme Court as a justification, one Federal District Court Judge in Pennsylvania held that no constitutional basis exists for any laws prohibiting the production and distribution of pornographic materials *(The United States vs. Extreme Associates 2005)*. This decision is just one example of what a lower federal court judge can attempt to impose on the rest of the country because of his interpretation of Supreme Court decisions. The judge wrote:

> *[W]e find that the federal obscenity statutes place a burden on the exercise of the fundamental rights of liberty, privacy and speech recognized by the Supreme Court.*

> *. . . we find that after Lawrence (Lawrence vs. Texas, 539 US 558) the government can no longer rely on the advancement of a moral code i.e., preventing consenting adults from entertaining lewd or lascivious thoughts, as a legitimate, let alone a compelling, state interest. (emphasis added)*

Happily this absurd decision was reversed on an appeal filed by the U.S. Department of Justice.

In testimony before the United States Senate Judiciary Committee, law professor William Wagner made the following statement:

> *In the federal judiciary's most recent results-driven analysis, the District Court, in U.S. vs. Extreme Associates (reversed on Appeal), created a new fundamental right to privacy for defendants in federal obscenity prosecutions. Creating this fundamental right enabled the Court to . . . strike down the Federal obscenity statutes as unconstitutionally violating the new fundamental right created by the court . . . [I]n divining this right hidden in the Constitution the court empowered itself to thereafter substitute its own public policy preferences for well-established choices previously made by the politically accountable branches of government. (Wagner)*

In a gathering of educators, lawyers, ecclesiastical leaders, and community activists held in Alexandria, Virginia, retired Appellate Justice Robert Bork referred to specific decisions of the Supreme Court as the "launching pad for every extreme philosophy intended to incite a cultural civil war in America." He quoted Supreme Court Justice Anthony Scalia as saying: "[D]ay by day, case by case, this court is designing a country that I do not recognize."

No Prosecution of Pornography under President Clinton

During the tenure of President Clinton, no efforts by the U. S. Department of Justice were made to prosecute the production and distribution of pornography. A senior official of the U.S. Department of Justice commented on my criticism of the Miller decision as follows:

> *I realize that the Miller test has failed this country in some respects. It would not have failed us to the same degree if prosecutors had aggressively prosecuted cases. The Clinton years were especially devastating – for twelve years, including the first term of George W. Bush, very few adult obscenity cases were brought to the court. That allowed the "community standard" to evolve unimpeded. (private letter)*

One of the important aspects of our strategy of using the public nuisance statutes in fighting pornography was the fact that these statutes gave the citizen the ability to fight against pornography when the responsible law enforcement officials declined to do so. However, in all fairness, the reticence of local prosecutors was not because they were sympathetic with obscenity. Ignoring pornographic films was simply an admission of the miserably complicated procedures that had to be followed to prosecute such pornography.

With their resources strained just to maintain basic law and order, it was simply not a priority to try to stop the exhibition of a motion picture, even one held as patently obscene by state and federal courts in other parts of the country. When a lone citizen began to utilize the available processes of the courts to fight a battle that the responsible law enforcement officials were hoping to ignore, they could no longer pretend that the nuisance was not there.

During Clinton's administration, Congress did enact several landmark statutes in an attempt to control the flood of obscene materials that began to appear on the internet. One example was the Child Pornography Prevention Act of 1996 that dealt with the production of child pornography by using adults who appear to be children. The statute also sought to restrict the use of computer imaging in the production of child pornography.

Those in the pornography industry provided ample funding to supposedly independent entities that assisted them in court to oppose such measures. The American Civil Liberties Union and the Free Speech Coalition are two such entities, whose efforts in the name of the First Amendment and "freedom of speech" were used against the Act, claiming it was unconstitutional by reason of vagueness.

In April 2002, the Supreme Court heard the case and struck down the statute. Dr. Robert Bork, a former federal appeals court judge and former Solicitor General for the United States who is widely acknowledged, even by those who disagree with him, as one of the most brilliant legal minds and jurists of this century, wrote a guest editorial for *The Wall Street Journal* commenting on the court's decision. Dr. Bork effectively summarized the paucity of legal rationale in this decision and many others in which the Court dealt with the issue of "free speech." Some extracts from his editorial follow:

The Supreme Court is not testing the limits of free "speech" so much as it is obliterating them. . . .

To anyone not familiar with the courts extraordinarily permissive rulings in the past, it might seem that any depiction of children in a variety of sexual acts could be prohibited. The government, however, was limited by [prior Supreme Court rulings] to arguing on grounds that virtually ensured its defeat.

The importance of [this] decision is less in its particular rejections of the government's necessarily limited rationales, however, than in the light the case throws upon the entire direction of First Amendment decisions that have brought the court to this point. There was, to put the matter bluntly, no good reason to throw free speech protections around pornography, nude dancing, raw profanity, and calls for law violation in the first place. Our jurisprudence has gone so far astray that there appears to be a right to display a picture of the Virgin Mary festooned with pornographic pictures and cow dung; but the presence of a creche on government property is a forbidden establishment of religion under the same amendment.

There is nothing in the First Amendment that requires these results. . . . [F]ar from enhancing the value of thought . . . the reduction of speech to the barracks-room level actively destroys thought that displays any subtlety, gradation, or nuance. All that is protected is the right of the individual to satisfy his desires, no matter how base, without regard to the rights of others or the health of the society. (Bork, 2002, p. A22)

Of course, not all opposition to the suppression of pornography comes from mean-spirited hypocrites such as some attorneys who defend the pornographers. Serious and credible arguments exist to support the concept of being on guard against the loss of essential liberties, of which freedom of speech is the foundation.

What zealots of anti-censorship rarely seem to grasp, however, is how quickly and effectively pornography crosses the line into that which has no legitimate right for protection. The vast majority of people in this country do not realize the extreme nature of the material that is now readily available.

With regard to the issue of "censorship" and the First Amendment, Bork, ever the scholar but also the keen observer of democratic institutions, wrote:

> *It will be said that to propose banning anything that can be called "expression" is an attempt to "take away our constitutional rights."* . . . *Until quite recently, nobody even raised the question of [the First] Amendment in prosecutions of pornographers; it was not thought relevant even by the pornographers. As late as 1942, in the Chaplinsky decision, a unanimous Supreme Court could agree:*

> *"There are certain well-defined and narrowly limited classes of speech, the prevention and punishment of which have never been thought to raise any Constitutional problems. These include the lewd and obscene, the profane, the libelous, and the insulting or 'fighting' words—those which by their very utterance inflict injury or tend to incite an immediate breach of the peace. It has been well observed that such utterances are no essential part of any exposition of ideas, and are of such slight social value as a step to truth that any benefit that may*

be derived from them is clearly outweighed by the social interest in order and morality."

. . . Yet it is clear that if there is something special about speech, something that warrants a constitutional guarantee, it is the capacity of speech to communicate ideas. . . . The only difference between speech and other behavior is speech's capacity to communicate ideas in the effort to reach varieties of truth. Celebration in song of the ripping of vaginas or forced oral sex or stories depicting the kidnapping, mutilation, raping, and murder of children do not, to anyone with a degree of common sense, qualify as ideas." (Bork, 1996, pp. 147–48)

Obscenity and pornography never present ideas except as a camouflage for the presentation of the obscene material. Sometimes defenders of pornography will attempt to conceal their vile presentations under the guise of the expression of "love," but the real intent is clearly to arouse lust and passion. Anyone who has viewed pornography even in its most elementary forms soon realizes it is the exact opposite of the expression of genuine affection, tenderness, or other human emotions consistent with love.

The most frequent form of elementary pornography is the graphic depiction of the human genitals. Nothing in such depictions convey any human emotions defensible as essential to the bonding of a man and woman. The women and men depicted in such exhibitions are in fact denigrated into subhuman objects for exploitation. In the more vicious forms of pornography, extreme violence and brutalization combined with bizarre sexual conduct quickly follows in the footsteps of the more elementary forms of obscenity.

Thus, the third mega-trend that has changed our culture is that the United States Supreme Court has been discarding centuries of legal tradition based on the assumption that Judeo-Christian values serve as the standard for human behavior. In an attempt to define pornography, it inadvertently handicapped state and local law enforcement teams from prosecuting an increasing stream of obscenities pouring into our cities and states.

And so the alienation of the upcoming generation continues unimpeded.

Chapter 5

Mega-trend #4:
THE VAST ECONOMIC COMPLEX THAT PROFITS
FROM PORN ADDICTION

According to an Omaha television station, a man sentenced to five to ten years in state prison for forcible rape had gone "from porn to prison."

"First it was *Playboy* that his father had brought into the home," KETV 7 reported. "Then it was the more graphic pornography magazines. Soon 'that wasn't enough.' Then it was videos, and then the Internet." On the Internet, the man began contacting women in chat rooms. He soon lost interest in his wife and family and began having sexual encounters with women online.

Finally one night he secretly met one of these women. In his interview he said, "I wanted what I wanted when I wanted it" (KETV 7, Omaha, Nebraska). Now he has five to ten years in the state penitentiary to ponder his path from porn to prison.

The obvious question is how could this man's father have been so inane as to bring a pornographic magazine into his home where a young son could find it?

I believe an experience I had recently is related. I attended a church service away from my local congregation, and on the bench in front of me sat a sweet family of four. A daughter about eight years of age became restless, so her mother handed her a magazine apparently published for her age group.

It was partially a coloring book and partially filled with photographs idolizing the fashions and lives of female artists who sing on MTV. A variety of credible surveys report this channel as the most popular with American teenagers. Yet, nearly all lyrics presented on this channel are vile renditions of sexual perversions, and the performers on MTV are known to engage openly in sexually arousing conduct.

So there I sat, watching a mother in a church meeting hand her little daughter a coloring book specifically designed to seduce young girls into believing that the way to be popular and attractive to men is to adopt fashions and behavior with pornographic overtones. I don't know where that mother obtained such a coloring book, but she obviously had no clue as to its real purpose nor did she understand what effect it could have on her presently innocent daughter.

From "porn to prison," from coloring books to immodest dress to promiscuity to unwed pregnancy. That pattern has been documented thousands – tens of thousands – of times, all part of the tragedy of the carnality and hedonism that is the harvest of America's newfound obsession with sex.

The Birth of the Sex Industrial Complex

Magazines and coloring books are two of thousands of products available that invite individuals into the "sex for recreation" mindset. Thousands more cater to those who have already been drawn into such a lifestyle, while the most disgusting products are sought by addicts whose appetites for sadistic perversions are never satisfied.

As in any industry, a large network of businesses and people help to design, produce, market, and distribute these products. Several years ago, the Lighted Candle Society published the book *The Sex Industrial Complex*. Its title was based on the phrase "Defense Industrial Complex," used by President Eisenhower in an address to the nation that he gave in 1960, the last year of his term. We selected this title because the primary message of our book was to warn the uninformed about the financial power, the political influence, and the subtle but devastatingly effective use of the entertainment industry enjoyed by the producers and distributors of pornography.

The Sex Industrial Complex emerged from the commercialization of the writings of various disciples of humanism and secularism, such as Marx, James, Dewey, Kinsey, and others whose philosophies deny the existence of moral absolutes. From their viewpoint, no evil exists, so there can be no good. Without good and evil, no overarching rules involving private conduct exist since no consequences for breaking such rules can exist.

The Sex Industrial Complex is made up of those who are willing to commercially exploit the philosophy that there should be no restraints on human passion short of denying anyone else the ability to give free rein to his or her own desires, appetites, and passions. Its ultimate purpose is money and power. Huge fortunes can be made by exploiting man's most base instincts – pornography serving only one. Forbes Magazine estimated a decade ago that the "sex industry" was worth close to sixty billion dollars per year worldwide.

Pornography publishers such as Hugh Hefner, Larry Flint, and their imitators creatively fashioned so-called "sophisticated legalisms" to enable the dismantling of laws and values that had been the basis of western society for centuries. Dr. Judith Reisman, in her book *Kinsey, Crimes & Consequences,* summed it up this way:

> *Kinsey's personal motive for his research was no mystery. He hated the way America's Christian-based law constrained America's sexual and moral life . . . We now know that Kinsey was not a lone researcher pursuing a perverse personal*

87

agenda. Rather, he operated with a vortex of such privileged and often inter-locked power brokers that their covert special interest agents stopped a Congressional investigation cold. (Reisman, 164)

During the 1960s and '70s the Sex Industrial Complex, through the American Legislative Council (ALEC), was able to remove hundreds of laws from federal and state civil and criminal codes restricting sexual behavior, most of which existed to protect women, children, and families from sexual exploitation. The "no fault" divorce laws that spread across the country are one classic example. The trivialization of rape and incest are other examples.

Within the Sex Industrial Complex, the entertainment industry helped mobilize the public news media to place Kinsey and his supposed "science" on a pedestal of absolute authority regarding the role of unrestrained sex. Meanwhile, certain magazine publishers as well as the music industry moved Americans incrementally towards a more sexualized culture. (The financial ties between the pornography industry and the music industry are well known and can be discovered by anyone who cares enough to research the facts.) The American Civil Liberties Union (ACLU), as a supposedly independent entity committed to protecting the First Amendment, was often brought in and continues to appear in courts all over the country to oppose any effort to restore and enforce family-friendly laws.

In the last two decades, the pay-per-view cable and satellite broadcasting industries have enabled the Sex Industrial Complex to operate directly inside the home. The video game producers, the big hotel chains, and the pharmaceutical industry's "pill" and other sexually enhancing products have also become part of this worldwide combination of financial powers motivated by the incredible financial rewards that come from the commercial exploitation of sex.

How the Sex Industrial Complex Works

An illustration of how the powerful Sex Industrial Complex works was experienced by the author of the following letter:

> *As I am usually a big fan, I flew to Chicago to attend a taping of Oprah's show. Initially it was very exciting and fun, but once they announced the topic that excitement turned to disappoint and embarrassment. The topic was, "How to Spice up Your Sex Life." During this show they had "experts" and doctors prescribing pornographic erotica to improve one's sex life. . . . The show went from bad to worse as Oprah posited that erotica and pornography could be acceptable and her guests encouraged people to use porn. I definitely wanted her to take a stand, and was shocked she didn't. (Letter to author)*

What "shocked" this correspondent is easily explained. The Oprah Winfrey show is owned by a private company called Harpo Productions, Inc. The financial success of that company depends upon the support of their advertisers for the Oprah Winfrey show. Among those advertisers are powerful businesses that participate in the Sex Industrial Complex. The topic for that show was likely dictated by those advertisers. The content of the show had one purpose only: to persuade the viewing audience that barnyard and back alley sexual conduct is a sure formula for a happy life.

Among Oprah's other advertisers who profit from this shameless mentality have been Pfizer (maker of Viagra), HBO (producer and distributor of pornography), and McDonalds (among the largest promoters of rap entertainers, many of whose obscene lyrics and pornographic videos are adulated by today's American teenagers).

In response to a letter criticizing their sponsorship of the show, one of the other advertisers on Oprah, Dove, gave this mindless testimonial: "We feel that the inspiring content on this site, its warm voice and constant encouragement for users to 'live their best lives' align amazingly well with our brand." I wonder if those who work for Dove agreed with the "sexpert" whose comment on Oprah was that open marriages (where partners feel free to engage in sex with anyone else) are the "happiest" marriages.

Every day, American television programs are shown whose only purpose is to promote the acceptance of shameless immorality. These messages first appeared on network programs quite subtly, but they soon evolved into open advocacy of unrestrained lustful behavior. Why did television go this direction?

1. Our culture has become so desensitized to sexually explicit materials in all media that a pervasive attitude of apathy exists towards efforts to thwart the spread of pornography through legislative and judicial initiatives.
2. The Sex Industrial Complex is so powerful and so skillful in manipulating the media, elected officials, and public opinion that the rank and file citizens who are trying to fight against the tsunami of smut finally wear out and disappear.
3. The number of people now willfully consuming pornography has reached a critical mass, creating an obstacle to efforts by local governments to respond to complaints by the minority against the presence of pornography.
4. Non-government community action groups who provide leadership for fighting the effects of pornography depend upon monetary contributions from the public to sustain their work. These contributions have never been adequate and continue to dwindle.
5. Our commitment to decency and dignity, once the essence of the American society, has been eroded. The family unit as the foundation of the nation's moral strength has been so

weakened that sufficient strength of character to rise up and fight back is lacking.

The Growth of Porn as an Industry

In the 1960s and '70s, what we regarded as the "hard core" pornography business in the United States was barely one-twentieth the size it is today. It was controlled by organized crime, and its products were mainly 8 mm black and white motion pictures produced in shabby warehouses in New York City or Los Angeles, along with pulp magazines with no dates on the cover.

A copy of a 1978 FBI report entitled "The Extent of Organized Crime Involvement in Pornography" was given to me by an FBI agent with whom I often collaborated in Los Angeles. The report was the work of field agents in fifty-nine U. S. cities where elements of organized crime were known to be operating. It was part of a major effort by the FBI to identify key individuals in the production and distribution of pornography throughout the country.

This report concluded that the involvement of organized crime in pornography was "indeed significant" and that "few pornographers can operate in the United States independently without some involvement with organized crime." Finally, it recommended that only "a well-coordinated all-out national effort from investigative and prosecutive forces" had a chance of stopping the spread of pornography, and that it was worth doing, "even if there is community apathy toward pornography.*"*

The apathy of the general public regarding obscenity encouraged those who produced and distributed it to become determined to produce motion pictures that were compatible for projection in motion picture theaters. An unfortunate decision by the U.S. Supreme Court that created a distinction between "adult pornography" and "child pornography" opened the door, and soon

91

the sex industry was producing large screen motion pictures for "adult" entertainment" at "adult" theaters.

In that same decade, the fashion industry began taking a major role in the Sex Industrial Complex, continuing a campaign to change the image of the ideal woman from a family nurturer to a competitor whose knowledge of sexual allurement was of far greater value than emotional succor. Various other elements of corporate America also became and have remained active participants in the desensitizing process that has brought us to the brink of a saturation of cultural obscenity.

During the decade of the eighties, technology allowed production of videocassettes. This gave the pornography industry the ability to market directly into the home, which brought an end to organized crime's monopoly control of the production and distribution of obscenity. In order to compete, magazines had to come out from under the counter. They began to appear in every grocery store at eye level for anyone six years of age or older, carrying one basic message: the ultimate female attribute is sexuality.

By this time, the pornography industry was financed openly by Wall Street. Multi-million dollar production budgets ended crude productions. Porn stars began to receive the highest awards of the motion picture industry. The most admired of Hollywood's glamour queens and kings flaunted conventional dignity by openly cohabiting and conceiving children out of wedlock.

De Facto Legalization of Pornography

But a much more fundamental change took place after 1989 when the administration of Ronald Reagan ended. Throughout the years and the nation, many voices of warning had either been ignored or had been given only the most begrudging nod of approval. For example, in 1972 the legislature and people of California rejected a proposed revision in their laws that could have prevented much of the production and distribution of obscenity in that state. Ten years later, the legislature and people of Utah did exactly the same thing.

On both occasions the people were deceived by massive propaganda campaigns financed by the Motion Picture Producers Association of America (MPAA) and such cable T.V. entities as HBO. In other words, the massive advertising campaigns that convinced voters to reject stronger laws designed to protect their society and their families were paid for by those who produce and distribute pornography.

Now what the FBI report had referred to as "community apathy toward pornography" helped to create a *de facto* legalization of pornography in America. In 1993, Janet Reno, President Clinton's newly appointed Attorney General of the United States, instructed the 92 U.S. Attorneys throughout the nation that they were not to prosecute any pornography cases. For the next eight years, the sex industry had an open license to produce and distribute pornography with no need to fear any effort by the nation's chief law enforcement officials.

Meanwhile, the decade of the nineties also introduced the Internet, which the pornography industry quickly co-opted. Visits to pornography websites outnumbered all others by a factor of ten to one. Law enforcement officials literally abandoned any effort to enforce laws intended to protect the last vestiges of dignity and morality in society. Many of those who could have and should have sounded the alarm pretended not to see the desolation that widespread pornography was now bringing into marriages and families.

Google and Microsoft introduced software features that helped people go to pornography websites without being detected by their employers or spouses. As one industry newsletter put it, "People in the industry are naming the feature 'porn mode' as it gives users the ability to view adult sites without leaving evidence."

An article in the *Edmonton Sun* noted the obvious hypocrisy involved as both Google and Microsoft attempted to justify these products by asserting that they allowed people to keep their "surfing private while using public computers." The reporter commented, "*We all know what the majority of folks are going to use this for. Might as well just call it Porn Mode and be done with it*" (Monday September 8, 2008).

A July 2008 report from Tom Johansmeyer's column noted that the pornography industry had just had another member of the Sex Industrial Complex obtain public financing: "Adult entertainment just got a new publicly traded player, Adult Entertainment Capital, Inc., and the flesh biz just moved a step closer to legitimacy." Mr. Johansmeyer's article went on to note, "For the past year and a half, we have seen finance creep into porn. AdultVest launched with endless fanfare and now claims it has access to $11 billion in investable assets, all to be used for the commercial production of pornography" (http://www.alleyinsider.com).

Half a dozen entities that are primarily engaged in the production and distribution of pornography are publicly traded on major stock exchanges. In addition, many of the major producers and distributors of pornography receive financial support and use the influence of major corporate entities.

A new and surprising face of the Sex Industrial Complex might soon be daily and weekly newspapers. For the past decade, as people have found more efficient ways to get their news, newspaper subscriptions have been dwindling. In an article in the E *Courant Electronic Edition*, Laurence Cohen suggested that supposedly dignified daily newspapers are seriously considering using pornography to save their empires from going defunct.

"The trick is to ease into the business gradually," wrote Mr. Cohen, "dabbling with porn in the print version of the newspapers to prepare the readers for what is to come. . . . Anyone who has traveled outside the United States, particularly in Western Europe, has seen for many years vile obscenity in the national newspapers of Europe" (August 29, 2008). He used *The Washington Post* as an example of "this grand endeavor," recalling "a front-page story about how young suburban girls were engaging in casual oral sex, as opposed to writing mushy notes to the cute boys in class." The *Post* was careful to write the initial story as a dull sociology text to avoid accusations that it had bumped something more important off the front page.

By the beginning of the 21st century, the will to enforce the laws that were already on the books had disappeared from most state and local law enforcement offices. Most local officials who wanted to do what the law mandated to protect society from the obscene could not get the financial support from the legislative bodies that controlled their budgets. By then many entities within the Sex Industrial Complex had amassed such power that they could intimidate or remove from office even the most determined law enforcement officials who attempted to prosecute the production and distribution of pornography.

In January 2009, the Lighted Candle Society hosted a delegation from Indonesia who came seeking assistance for stemming the flood of obscene materials that were wreaking tragic consequences among the Muslim youth of their nation. Meanwhile, social commentators in Great Britain, Germany, and Eastern Europe reported the abysmal epidemic of sexual conduct among their youth.

In Russia, addiction to pornography surpassed alcohol addiction as the most devastating vice among young people. Even in China, where seven decades of totalitarian government control over all media production and distribution made the presence of pornography extremely rare, the Internet opened society to the rapidly increasing presence of the obscene.

The MPAA and the ACLU

Certain groups have been especially aggressive in broadening public access to pornography. One of those groups is the Motion Picture Association of America (MPAA). In 1968, as a member of the California State Senate, I introduced legislation (SB 372) that would create an entity in the state government called The California Motion Picture Review Board. This Board would have the responsibility of objectively rating motion pictures on the basis of their suitability for family viewing.

The MPAA moved quickly to defeat the proposed legislation. When the bill passed the state Senate, they brought in their most powerful lobbyists, and when it appeared that the bill would also pass the other house in California's legislature, the MPAA came forward with an alternate proposal. If the legislature would defeat my bill, they (the MPAA) would create a rating entity within the industry. All costs associated with the rating system would be paid for within the industry.

It did not require any great depth of intellect to see the obvious: the fox was offering to guard the henhouse at no expense to the owner of the chickens. I warned my colleagues that the MPAA would simply distort the rating system and use it for their own benefit. With the effective use of money and prostitutes, the motion picture industry's titans defeated my bill.

Over the next four decades, what I predicted is exactly what happened. The MPAA has consistently manipulated the rating system, using it as a means of assisting in the marketing of motion pictures. No serious effort appears to be made by the review board to protect children and youth from exposure to images that are unsuitable for young impressionable minds.

In fact, some producers and scriptwriters have been specifically instructed to include certain scenes in a motion picture to justify a rating that would tweak the audience's interest in the prurient content of the picture. Slowly but ever spiraling downward, their rating system has legitimized the exhibition of sexually explicit images to children of all ages.

In 1985 President Ronald Reagan instructed the Attorney General of the United States to create a Commission on Pornography. Two years later, when the Commission's report was issued, the President of the MPAA hired the most powerful and expensive public relations firm in Washington, D.C. to denigrate the findings. In a memorandum written prior to the publication of the Commission's report, Robert Gray, the CEO of the firm, set forth the following strategy:

> *Quiet efforts should be undertaken to persuade the Attorney General, the White House, and the leaders of both political parties that the forthcoming report of work of the Commission is so flawed, so controversial, so contested and so biased that they should shy away from publicly endorsing the document. The more doubts that can be created about the objectivity and validity of the Commission's findings and recommendations, the more difficult it will be for anti-pornography crusaders to use the report as an effective tool for achieving their objectives.*

After the report was issued, another official of the Gray Public Relations firm admitted,

> *"We attempted to call into question the motives, motivation, the values of the people on the Commission,*

raise questions about their own backgrounds. Tried to shoot holes in the report itself, and in the hearing process."

With enormous financial resources at their disposal, the MPAA succeeded. Stories that asserted the Commission's report was scientifically invalid were planted in the nation's most highly regarded newspapers and magazines. Members of the Senate and the House of Representatives publicly raised doubts about the report and its validity. For many years it was almost impossible to get a copy of the report (now available on the Internet at http://www.porn-report.com/).

MPAA remains one of the principle participants in the Sex Industrial Complex. Other contributors include such "respectable" entities as Rupert Murdock's Newscorp, the major hotel chains, Comcast and AT&T, Time-Warner, magazine publishers, the largest most powerful elements of the music industry, video-game manufacturers, some of the largest retailers in the country, and television and cable television producers and distributors.

The MPAA, along with the television industry, has consistently provided legal support for pornographers through the American Civil Liberties Union (ACLU) by making sure the ACLU has enough financial resources to consistently "volunteer" to defend producers and distributors of pornography in both the courts and the legislative chambers.

No organization has been more aggressive in defending the actions of the pornography industry than the ACLU. It was in the forefront of Roth's defense, and it was ever present in all of our courtroom battles, acting as "amicus" or "friend of the court" petitioners on behalf of the pornographers. Whether the judges and juries truly believed this pretended separation of interests was never certain, but more often than not it worked. Never mind that the majority of

ACLU financing came from the very people who were producing and distributing the pornography.

Note the following statements of policy taken from the ACLU official *Policy Guide*:

The ACLU opposes any restraint on the right to create, publish or distribute materials to adults, or the right of adults to choose the material they read or view, on the basis of Obscenity, Pornography or Indecency.

Laws which punish the distribution or exposure of such material to minors violate the First Amendment and inevitably restrict the right to publish and distribute such materials to adults. . . . The ACLU maintains that a causal relationship between exposure to sexually explicit material and juvenile delinquency has never been carried (sic) to the point of definitive proof . . . the First Amendment does not allow suppression of speech because of the potential harm . . . (6th revised *Policy Guide,* ACLU, June 1986)

The arguments in support of the pornographers were always couched in language involving the First Amendment rights of freedom of speech. As many a courageous dissenting judge noted, no one could remotely conceive of a loss of free speech through the restriction of the production and distribution of this vile material. Still, the downhill slide seemed destined to accelerate and it continues unabated.

What "ideas" is it so critical for the ACLU to protect? The presentations the ACLU wanted to protect for their financial supporters included the most deviant and perverted of sexual conduct, often associated with sadomasochistic violence. There were no "ideas" in danger of suppression, only the degenerate, vulgar, crude exploitation of sexual deviancy.

Judge Robert Bork commented:

The head of the ACLU announced in a panel discussion that the Supreme Court's failure to throw protection around nude dancing in night clubs was a terrible blow to our freedom of speech. Some years back, when I suggested to a law school audience that the courts had gone too far in preventing communities from prohibiting pornography, the then president of the organization (ACLU) compared me to Salazar of Portugal and the Greek Colonels. Afterward he said he had called me a fascist. It is fascinating that when one calls for greater democratic control and less governance by a judicial oligarchy, one is immediately called a fascist. The ACLU seems to think democracy is tyranny and government by judges is freedom. (Bork, 1996, p. 153).

So in addition to the enormous financial returns obtained from pornography by the Sex Industrial Complex, another highly motivating reason for continuing what they are doing is the lust for power. Addiction to pornography gives the producers and distributors of pornography enormous power – power over the individual addict as well as financial resources that give them power over communities, over other institutions (such as research carried out at academic institutions), and even over judges and our government itself. When such power reaches a critical mass, it can overthrow the constitutional protections that our founding fathers created when they founded our Republic.

Competition from Amateur Pornographers

Thus the war against perversion and the subversion of the moral heritage of our nation goes on. In that war we are still losing ground

The "adult entertainment industry," as pornographers now refer to themselves, keep a close watch on the dollar sales volume for their products. For instance, the year 2010 saw a record-breaking production of pornographic DVDs and videocassettes in the United States. Still, commercial producers and distributors of pornography became concerned at an overall decrease in revenue from their main sources of income: "pay per view" cable and satellite sales, the DVD and videocassette sales, and credit card sales over the Internet for obscene materials. While sales grossed more than $14 billion in 2011, they were down nearly a billion dollars from the year before.

If we were to assume that this loss of revenue came about because people were finally awakening to the tragedies that inevitably follow porn addiction, we would be disappointed. The loss of revenue was due to a huge increase in the number of "amateurs" who are now producing and distributing explicit sexual materials. Literally thousands of individuals who have video cameras and need only recruit two or more people willing to engage in sex before the camera can produce competing products and sell them on the Internet. Some of these "amateur" producers don't even attempt to obtain income, but make pornographic products simply to outdo other amateurs for viewer approval of their depraved content.

The pornography industry's established producers have reacted by spending millions of dollars on new technologies that they think will ultimately win back the audience now patronizing "amateur" sites. Two major efforts in this regard are "interactive" pornography and "video on demand" pornography. The first allows the consumer to actually participate in scenes they can project in their homes or hotel rooms via a receiver as small as a cell phone.

Research for "video on demand" technology is being carried out that will make it possible for a viewer to call up any currently popular porn star and dictate the various type of sexual conduct they want to see. Viewers will also be able to include themselves in the audio/visual scenario. Major producers in the porn industry are confident that this interactive technology along with the "video on demand" aspect will result in pornography so realistic that the market for the current flood of amateur productions will disappear, or at least be kept to a minimum.

Pornography at the Movies

An especially troubling development became public in Europe in June 2007. The European Commission launched its own channel on YouTube. It contained various videotaped messages about climate change, human rights, and humanitarian aid. One site was entitled, "Film Lovers Will Love This!"

Clicking on the title took the viewer to a series of clips showing 18 different couples, both homosexual and heterosexual, having sex in a variety of settings. Commission spokesman, Martin Selmayr, said the shots were drawn from award-winning films made in Europe: "[T]hese highlighted Europe's tradition of rich cinema." Selmayr also asserted he had not received any complaints about the video even though a variety of European lawmakers had expressed strong disapproval.

In the first week of broadcasting, the site with graphic sexual content received 280,000 visits while the humanitarian aid site, which had the next highest number of visits, received a total of 18,000. More than fifteen times as many people were viewing the graphic sexual content sites as opposed to learning how to participate in humanitarian aid projects. What must we conclude about the success of the war against pornography when these numbers are considered?

Since a single type of image doesn't satisfy the pornography addict for long, producers and distributors of pornography have continually sought for other ways to satisfy the addict's craving for material that is "more and more deviant." The Sex Industrial Complex found a willing ally in the appalling allure of horror films until the two have finally merged into what is referred to as the "torture porn" or "horror porn" genre.

Here is a sample description of a scene from such a film: "The girl is gagged, tied, and naked, hanging upside down in a dark and cavernous chamber. She's bleeding – her throat has been cut. She's still alive but slowly dying. Her blood pours out all over her murderer, who lies beneath her drinking her blood and bathing in it."

In another of the torture porn films, victims are eaten by their murderers – copied from the real life story of one pornography addict's history of serial killings. Scenes similar to these, far too sick to be described here, are becoming the typical fare in popular theaters around the country. What was once reserved only for the sleeziest of "adult" theaters and back alley hideaways is now conceived, financed, and distributed by major motion picture studios.

When asked to explain how such a switch could happen so quickly, one Hollywood executive explained:

> *It's a change of attitude, really, and perspective. It used to be that the studio heads and the kind of grownup public in general were not familiar with horror films and thought they were something nasty and kind of sick. Now a lot of the studio heads and critics and everybody else have grown up watching the genre and they think . . . "we're nasty and sick!" But that is good; so there's a lot more openness to it.*

When the nation was shocked in 2004 with revelations about the conduct of U.S. soldiers at the Abu Ghraib prison in Iraq, the "alien" generation of which those soldiers were part were perplexed at what the fuss was about. After all, they had been watching that sort of thing on the motion picture screen for years. One porn horror film producer simply observed:

[S]ex is not new, torture is not new. Both of them have been a form of entertainment for years. We have simply presented a vividly realistic form of sexual torture that that the audience has learned to believe is really happening in many places around the world.

Other producers of these films use an old rationale to justify what they are doing to our society. As one studio executive noted, "It goes without saying that throughout the history of the horror film there has always been a reflection in the films themselves of the times in which we live."

"Of course, this argument is used to validate the genre, to give it some kind of justification as a form of cultural expression," explained the Chair of Cinema Studies at Tisch School of the Arts at New York University. No doubt most of these films included an "alien" creature in the plot and other images capable of producing, in the psyche of the adolescents and young adults who patronized them, a callousness toward violence and graphic sex that helped to create the "alien" generation now in the early stages of adulthood.

In 2008, Bill Carroll, Katz Television Group's Vice President and Director of Programming, said, "Things that would not have been acceptable five or ten years ago in our society are considered just part of the ongoing culture today. Broadcast television reflects society."

From Parents Television Council:

Today's prime-time television programming is not merely indifferent to the institution of marriage and the stabilizing role it plays in our society, it seems to be actively seeking to undermine marriage by consistently painting it in a negative light .... [Our] study found nearly three times as many verbal references to non-marital sex compared to marital sex on the broadcast networks during the 2005 programming hours studied. . . . Visual references to . . . kinky sex, bondage, sadomasochism and prostitution outnumbered the same for marital sex nearly three to one.

Finally, from Forbes.com, in an article entitled "Sexing Up Prime Time," came this comment: "Networks face an onslaught of competition from steamy cable fare [and] are noticeably – and perhaps desperately – pushing the sexual envelope. Series like [names have been omitted] . . . are loaded with adulterous escapades and visuals to match."

Another industry publication lists thirty-four countries where the most sexually explicit network programs from the United States are broadcast on a regular basis. Thus, the United States has the distinction of not only creating and spreading social contagion among our own youth, but also exporting it to almost all nations throughout the world where broadcast television is available.

Video Games

Related to television programming and movies as a pornographic outlet for the Sex Industrial Complex is the industry surrounding video games. An ancient historian who recorded the moral decline of his own society by noting that their lustfulness and cruelty had degenerated to such a degree that "they were past all feeling" could well have been describing the content of today's games. They represent a major source of pornography for teenagers and young adults in America.. The content of violent sexual perversion in many of these "games" are ultimately leading many of those who indulge themselves in playing towards becoming true aliens.

One review of the most popular videogames in America refers to their sexualized imagery as "soft porn," but goes on to say:

> *However, the overtly sexual content of the games must be regarded as invariably leading the player to seek out the more graphic hard core versions of pornography that are so readily available.*

> *In many ways the sexual perversion and the violence contained in the videogames is more conducive to the player ultimately "acting out" the scenes portrayed in the games than might be expected from standard hard core pornography . . . The reason for this is the "interactive virtual reality" [where] the player is able to personally engage in the conduct shown in the game. The player inflicts the physical violence and the sexual behavior upon the victims (both men and women) shown in the game.*

> *[Typical of the games are] female characters [who] receive a tremendous beating at the hands of the male characters and other females depicted in the game . . . complete with blood spurting from wounds, screams and groans of pain, and the ultimate usually very gruesome death of the victim. All of this is controlled by the player of the game who in terms of "virtual reality" is actually inflicting the physical violence upon the victims.*

> *. . . [Some] games feature a female power role that regularly attacks and kills anything or anyone that may get in her way. . . . The typical female depicted in the games can be described as having exaggerated female legs,*

abdomen, and breasts, with an adolescent face similar to most Asian women. The women . . . end up nude, sometimes as part of the design of the game, and sometimes undressed at the will of the player. The games present an unattainable female stereotype in sexuality, as well as females who are physically aggressive and as strong as men. These women give and take the same constant physical abuse as their male counterparts.

. . . The 2003 edition of the Playboy video games and others like it all reward the game player with pornographic content. Many of the games reward correct answers to trivia questions with a video of spring break co-eds undressing and flashing their breasts while promoting drunken sexual activity. These games facilitate computer-generated sexual relations with both males and females, heterosexual or homosexual, according to the wishes of the game player.

Many of these games portray graphic violence of the most sadistic nature. . . . Prostitutes are commonly used in the games for sexual purposes and then for whatever reason are subjected to physical violence and ultimate death according to the wishes of the game player. There are no plain or average women in the games, just the voluptuous women with highly exaggerated bosoms.

Clinical psychologists have repeatedly warned that young men attracted to the sleek sexy creations of the videogame will inevitably become addicted to the real flesh versions that are available in cable television and Internet pornography. . . . In addition to the sexual perversions, these young minds have been filled with grizzly acts of savagery and physical brutality that they will always associate with any type of sexual experience. (Smith, 2003, used with permission)

More recent studies have confirmed that pornography addicts from 13 to 35 years in age are using the latest "interactive" videogames to have what is called a "virtual reality" sexual experience. The player of the game can deal with the animated young women portrayed by the software in whatever way he desires, engaging in any variety of sexual perversions with the fantasy girls and in an almost endless variety of types of physical abuse. Many of these games include cannibalistic rituals involving the dead body of the victim.

Making Halloween a Pornographic Holiday

Every October 31st billions of dollars are spent celebrating another event that has become an enormously profitable enterprise for the pornography industry. The horror movies and "haunted houses" that have become such an integral part of the Halloween celebration are saturated with sexually explicit scenes of torture and violence. People ought to be stunned at the vile nature of these virtual reality presentations.

During the media build-up to Halloween, commercials for local Haunted Houses have often featured a beautiful but terrified young woman being chased through the woods by a demonic ghoul. The commercial ends as the creature leaps onto a bed with the girl, who is screaming in horror. In essence, the message is, "This woman met a horrific death . . . See it close up in our Haunted House!"

The nationwide "haunted house" phenomenon follows on the heels of horror films containing brutality and torture that would make a gulag jailor recoil in disgust. Instead of trafficking in classic ghosts and witches, the skillfully crafted sets and stages graphically depict the dismemberment of human bodies and sometimes sexually explicit torture. Yet, children line up and pay to view this particularly desensitizing and dehumanizing savagery.

These scenes of brutality, murder, and sexual mayhem are made possible by using "simulation" technology. Each year, producers attempt to break new ground in the "simulated" display of the sordid and the sensational

However, the effect on the brains of the children and youth who are watching do not distinguish between "simulated" and actual. Step by step their brains becomes saturated with images of violence and sexual perversion that, as described in Chapter 1, can totally overwhelm the cognitive and inhibiting portions of the brain.

How can we expect our children to respect women and to protect human life when even once a year we join in a celebration that dwells on the macabre and mind-numbing brutality of *The Texas Chainsaw Massacre*? Compare the way today's television and movie stars vie with one another to attract attention with public conduct that is vulgar, immoral, indecent, and in every way lacking of any sense of dignity or shame with the following paragraph taken from the actual contract of Loretta Young, a well-known female star of motion pictures from the 1930s to the 1950s:

> *The artist agrees to conduct himself with due regard to public conventions and morals, and agrees that he will not do or commit any act or thing that will tend to degrade him in society or bring him into public hatred, contempt, scorn or ridicule, or that will tend to shock, insult or offend the community or ridicule public morals or decency....*

And so I once again pose the question: Are we all mad? Has our society so totally lost its moral bearings that there is nothing left that can shock us or offend what remains of our human sensitivities? How much farther must we descend into the depths of decadence until we begin to understand that how a society chooses to "entertain" itself cannot simply be dismissed with a shrug of the shoulders?

The generation being raised with this type of desensitizing brain washing is rapidly coming to power in our culture. Their numbers increase each year. What will the "aliens" that we have created do with regard to the senior members of society who because of the vicissitudes of age are no longer able to be productive? Will they even hesitate to dispose of older, no longer "useful" members of society? Will they feel any sense of loyalty to or gratitude for sacrifices made in their behalf by a now obsolete generation?

Not likely.

Within the Sex Industrial Complex, a critical mass of individuals has come together whose power and influence through mass media far exceed their numbers. They practice hedonism in its most extreme perversions. They acknowledge no restraints upon carnal behavior; nor do they recognize the existence of any laws higher than those prompted by the most base vulgarities.

In their pursuit of the huge financial profits that will continue to come from exploiting the weaknesses of our youth they are creating a generation of aliens who have lost all contact with the noble, the virtuous and the valiant qualities that have made us a nation.

We must respond! We must awaken the American people to the danger of the moral anarchy that will undoubtedly result if the present trends are not reversed.

Chapter 6

GRASPING THE EXTENT OF AMERICA'S
PORNOGRAPHY PROBLEM

Porn has always been around. However, the norms and structure of our society kept it limited in content and scope for almost 150 years. With the exception of a time in the 1890's in New York City, pornography was kept tightly concealed and its circulation contained.

New technologies that were developed during World War II began an era where printed pornography first began to reach inside of American homes. Still, the general public shared basic standards of behavior that directly and indirectly discouraged the kind of exposure to sexuality and violence that we now experience on a regular basis. At that time, the discovery that someone regularly viewed pornography meant embarrassment and shame, and possibly the loss of a job or public office.

By the early 1960s, when I became involved in the fight against obscenity, the main pornographic products were "slick" magazines and 8mm black and white motion pictures, all sold from "under the counter." Unfortunately, several inept decisions by the United States Supreme Court resulted in the proliferation of "adult" bookstores and movie theaters (see Chapter 4). With that increasing market came improved quality in both pornographic print and film.

The development of the videocassette and DVD finally made possible the pornographer's dream: the ability to market directly into the home without the consumer having to run the risk of purchasing pornography in public. Dedicated channels on cable and satellite television followed, and the market demand for obscenity soon pushed the production of hardcore pornographic films past ten thousand per year.

Relaxed Public Standards and More Technology

Subtle signs of relaxed public standards began to appear during the 70s, 80s, and 90s, such as the rejection of modesty in grooming and clothing fashions. Schoolteachers began showing up at class wearing jeans with T-shirts that propagandized the rejection of basic American culture. Students could only be distinguished from the teachers by their even more slovenly appearance. The fashion industry targeted ten- and eleven-year-old girls with the falsehood that their clothing had to be sexually alluring or their lives would be miserable.

Without a full realization of how they were being exploited, the rising generation began to reject and mock the values of dignity for which their parents had sacrificed. Some even took glee in burning the flag for which men and women who are buried in faraway places had made the ultimate sacrifice. For the first time, music became the chosen medium for vulgarity and rebellion. Whenever a religious leader, teacher, or occasional politician began to warn of the consequences to any society that engaged in the wholesale rejection of their cultural heritage, their warning voices were obscured by the surrounding prosperity.

The entrance of the Internet dissolved any ability to stop pornography in harbors and airports. Almost overnight, anyone anywhere on earth could produce and electronically distribute obscenity to everyone everywhere on earth.

Today, not only can almost everyone access pornography in the privacy of their own homes, they can do so in secrecy from others inside their homes via laptops and personal phones. With the emergence of the video cell phone, we now have children committing felonies by photographing their own private body parts and transmitting them to other children.

Thus, in the past half century, a nation that once held unusually high standards of decency, dignity, and morality, experienced the gradual erosion of any sense of shame. Thanks to a continuous stream of the vulgar, the profane, and the obscene – primarily accomplished through the entertainment and advertising media – the sexualization of our culture has corrupted even the most revered aspects of childhood.

How bad has it become? As far back as 1989, a Los Angeles Superior Court judge dismissed complaints against four pornographic films because, as he wrote: "I can not conclude that the films were patently offensive in an area as diverse as Los Angeles" (*Los Angeles Times,* Thursday, May 4, 1989). The four films included graphic depictions of group sex, oral sex, beatings and bondage, gang rape, and a woman committing suicide after she had been sexually attacked. "I cannot say beyond a reasonable doubt that community standards were violated," stated the judge.

Needless to say, the presence of pornography is much worse now than it was in 1989, even in Los Angeles. Currently its presence in the lives of Americans is more ubiquitous, disruptive, and dangerous than most people imagine.

Marketing Pornography to Women

Adults are already somewhat desensitized to sexually explicit materials because the subject matter is all about them. They can easily forget what might be happening in the mind of a nearby child. Marcia Herman-Giddens, a professor at the University of North Carolina at Chapel Hill, wrote:

I was recently standing at the checkout counter of the supermarket with my twelve-year-old granddaughter when I happened to notice that her eye level was exactly on level with the Cosmopolitan magazine. The headline on the cover was "10 Ways to Drive Your Man Wild in Bed" and my granddaughter was standing there, reading, looking at this half-naked woman. I'm thinking to myself, "I wonder what in God's name is going through this child's mind." It's in their face, all the time, literally. ("The Making of an 8-year-old Woman," The New York Times Magazine)

Beginning in the mid-1970's, members of the Sex Industrial Complex began systematically seeking to expand their consumer base to include more women. Girls in their mid- to late teens were especially targeted with campaigns asserting that romantic happiness was most readily found by women who engaged in sexual intimacy designed to gratify the carnal desires of "the typical man." Major pornography producers took out advertisements in glossy magazines for teens, promoting clothing that was sexually provocative. Articles began appearing in women's magazines that were increasingly satiated with erotic content.

In a western daily newspaper, I later read the review of a book written by an individual in her early thirties who had been deceived by this campaign. She recited how she had been persuaded by continuous presentations in movies, on television, and in magazines that unrestrained sexual permissiveness was indeed the secret to a fulfilling life. After many years of bitter disappointment, she finally came to the realization that the harvest in her life that came from sexual permissiveness was not one of happiness, but of despair.

The content and nature of today's magazines also show the incredible degree to which women themselves are contributing to the increased acceptance of pornography among women. A dozen or more magazines, written by and for women, have a predominant theme of sexual ecstasy. Their articles depict the supposed ease with which women may discard sexual inhibitions and find "fulfillment" (a term that pornographers have used and abused for decades) in sexual freedom. This incredible slide into the mire will only hasten the time when these readers will require more and more explicit sexual materials to satisfy their newfound appetite for the obscene.

A very active correlation exists between what "legitimate" media depicts and promotes as acceptable behavior and what pornographers initially present as "normal love-making." The process is ongoing in both the printed and motion picture media. The inevitable result and overt purpose is to create an increasing appetite for the obscene which, as it becomes more graphic, also becomes more expensive. Also, a pornographic product never becomes obsolete and has no shelf life, thus assuring the ultimate profitability of producing pornography.

Data from independent sources confirm that the sex industry's marketing strategy is succeeding. The daily fare of television "sex soap operas" has done much to entice women who might otherwise have remained aloof to become enmeshed in pornography's web. However, research indicates that it is mainly women in the workplace who are fueling the growth of pornographic consumption among women by using the Internet and "pay per view" adult films on cable television. According to an article in the *New York Times*:

> *While women have long been involved in the sex industry as providers and consumers, their participation now has become more of an economic phenomenon, largely because of the Internet. In fact, experts say, the Internet has been a major factor in unleashing women's interest in all things sexual.*

115

Surveys by Nielsen/Net Ratings, which measures Internet audience, have found that women account for more than a quarter of all visitors to sites with adult content. ComScore Media Metrix, an Internet research firm, has found even higher female demand for adult sites – 42% of all visitors in January – with the highest rate among women ages 18 to 34. (The New York Times, February 20, 2004)

The dramatic increase in the last twenty years of professional women who travel in their occupations has also increased the number of women who later seek therapeutic assistance in escaping the clutches of a pornography addiction. Across the United States, hotels are reporting that women clients are insistent upon having access to pornographic "pay per view" television. "Many guests are choosing the racy stuff," says Leonard Sabal, president of Cabil Corporation, which helps hotels bill for in-room entertainment. "It's a major business in the U.S. hotel market – approximately $500 million a year."

Meanwhile a poll conducted by "the world's most visited Christian website" asserts that a surprising number of women who regard themselves as "active practicing Christians" have become dependent upon pornography. The poll results were tallied from over one thousand self-selected responses and indicate that 20% of all Christian women are addicted to pornography, according to Clay Jones, President of Second Glance Ministries. The group defines "addicted" as "use on an ongoing basis."

Two researchers retained by the Lighted Candle Society visited a large city in the southeastern United States to meet with various therapeutic facility administrators and clinicians who handle sexual addictions. They were surprised at the vastly increased numbers of women coming to these clinics for help with regard to an addiction to pornography.

A Howard Center newsletter reported that a group of historians who met during a conference in Washington, D.C. raised this question: During the 20th century, what ideology/worldview was most influential in reshaping ideas, attitudes, and institutions?

> We considered the last flowering and then the ruin of monarchism in the fires of World War I, and the rise and eventual defeat of Fascism, Naziism, and Japanese Imperialism, the Bolshevik victory in Russia and the spread of Communism to Eastern Europe . . . the re-emergence of a militant Islam in the latter decades of the century, and so on. *But in the end, we concluded that the greatest success had been registered by a surprise candidate: the ideology known as liberal or equity feminism.* (_The Family In America_, November 2003; emphasis added)

The feminist movement itself has been influenced by and has functioned as an unintended ally of the Sex Industrial Complex. By denigrating the ideal of the traditional family, the separate but equal roles of husbands and wives in providing the nation with its most powerful stabilizing entity – the nuclear family – the feminist movement also aided in creating a market for pornography among women.

The irony is that no single force has done more to denigrate women than the Sex Industrial Complex. Its basic message from the start has been that women are objects, creatures to be exploited for the carnal satisfaction of men. What a travesty that so many women have bought into such a lie.

Teens and Pornography

The sexualization of today's teenage world has become painfully obvious. The sexual overtones of rock music and programs like MTV as well as the sexual violence of video games leave little doubt that many teens are drawn into an addiction to pornography. A less obvious catalyst has been school sex education programs which have introduced pre-teens and teenagers to subject matter that primes them for exploring pornography. In testimony of before the Massachusetts hearings on HB 1641, entitled *An Act to Provide For a Comprehensive Health Education Program in Public Schools,* Dr. Judith Reisman described the legislation as an "anti-child, anti-parent, anti-Judeo-Christian and anti-family" effort that would "stomp out traditional American views of sexuality in all school children." (Reisman, *Kinsey, Crimes & Consequences*).

Reisman also quoted the following from a booklet distributed nationwide to junior high school students: "If this is a girl you've just met and she agrees [to have sex], you're in the clear provided that she's old enough to have some sense. . . . Sex with victims is always wrong. Sex without is always right." From a "Position Statement" by SIECUS (Sex Information and Education Council of the U.S.) regarding materials suitable for use in providing sex education to schoolchildren, she also quoted this troubling sentence: "When sensitively used in a manner appropriate to the viewer's age and developmental level, sexually explicit visual, printed, or online materials can be valuable educational or personal aids helping to reduce ignorance and confusion and contributing to a wholesome concept of sexuality."

Sex education across the nation has been influenced by people like the leaders of Planned Parenthood, who have been quoted as saying, "Teachers and parents should help young people obtain sex satisfaction before marriage. By sanctioning sex before marriage, we will prevent fear and guilt." Faye Wattleton, a past Planned Parenthood President, was quoted in the *Los Angeles Times* as saying, "We've got to be more concerned about how to prevent teen pregnancies than we are about stopping sexual relationships."

Public libraries can also be problematic in terms of refusing to protect teenagers from pornography. In Cleveland, Ohio, "a man was arrested for masturbating while on the computer in the children's department at the Cleveland Public Library." The same individual had been arrested six months earlier "for downloading child pornography at the Mayfield Village Library" (*WKYC.com.* Cleveland, April 10,2003).

In spite of incidents like the above, the American Library Association and the American Civil Liberties Union (ACLU) continue to do everything in their power to frustrate, oppose, and overturn any legislative enactment, federal or state, that would require public libraries to install filters on their computers and to monitor the activities of young people using the computers.

The case of a county librarian in Weber County, Utah, came to my attention. She had observed a young patron accessing pornography on the Internet and immediately ordered him to close the pornography site. When he refused to do so, she simply shut off the computer. The next day she reported the incident to the executives of the county library board responsible for handling such an incident. In her letter she also documented how she was continually required to deal with such problems when junior high and high school students used the library computers to access Internet pornography.

In her repot she asked the library board to take more effective action to prevent the unsupervised use of the library terminals by young people who view pornography. She also raised the issue as to why the board had never complied with the state statute requiring libraries to install filtering devices on their computers.

Ten days after having written her letter, this employee was given a notice of dismissal. In response to her request for legal assistance, David Jordan, a former U.S. Attorney was retained to represent her. The evidence gathered by her, Jordan, and others confirmed that the use of library computers for access to Internet pornography was rampant throughout the entire state. Further, the American

Library Association had used various means to circumvent complying with state statutes requiring filters.

As the litigation process went forward, the county used the tactic of repeated interrogations and depositions to exhaust the employee's emotional and financial ability to pursue the matter. She simply could not afford to continue taking time off from her new employment to deal with the legal manipulations. Her lawsuit against the county was settled out of court. And the librarians continue to ignore the laws.

The Sex Industry – Targeting Minors

When it comes to making money on minors by targeting them as a market that can be drawn into pornography, there is simply no longer any sense of shame.

Entities like Playboy talk about "stretching" their "carefully selected and well-coordinated brand licensing" down to "the next generation." This includes selling Playboy sponsored games for mobile devices to attract young boys as well as cute little "bunny" accessories to little girls. As Christi Hefner, the former CEO of Playboy, put it, the company was an "early believer in extending the brand," including the bunny which "is a valuable trademark," supposedly because of the lifestyle it represents. (Stuart Mil, http://www.multichannel.com/article/CA6570421.html, July 24, 2008)

Playboy likes to partner with Spencers Gifts, a firm based in New Jersey with over 650 retail outlets throughout the United States. While Spencers' target market is the teen-age and pre-teenage group (local store managers have been instructed to hire sales persons as young as local statutes and ordinances allow), their inventory for the last thirty years has consistently included sexually explicit merchandise.

Although some Spencers stores have been cited by local law enforcement officials for displaying and selling obscene materials to minors, most get away with selling a wide selection of brothel paraphernalia in store and online without the required age verification, such as "stripper poles" (Spencer's buyer comments include descriptions of how girlfriends were encouraged to strip and perform), various representations of male genitalia, large posters of bare-breasted women fondling each other's genitals underneath scanty briefs, and various manuals on sexual intercourse.

Public display of such sex tools (deliberately and fraudulently called "toys") inadvertently supports a sex predatory criminal subculture where child victims of sexual abuse are entrapped using such Spencer's trivializing sex tools as fluffy handcuffs and posters of public sex images. These items are also used by predators to legitimize to their young victims what they do.

One does not need to return to an earlier century to note that moral public nuisances like Spencers and Playboy Enterprises has contributed to the fact that our social environment now includes the incredible increases in sexually transmitted diseases, youth suicide, illegitimacy, abortion, violent crimes like rape and child abuse.

Pornography and Crimes Against Children

One day when passing an advertising billboard that urged the local citizenry to petition their legislature to make cruelty to animals a felony, I remembered a conversation I once had with a senior executive in a major advertising firm. I proposed that the Lighted Candle Society should pay to rent some billboards carrying a warning about pornography. Even though we offered to pay the standard rate for the billboards, we were turned down. When I pursued the issue of why we were turned down, I was told that it was not because our message wasn't true or because it was too strident. We were turned down because the pornography industry had the capability to financially destroy any outdoor advertising company that would agree to post our message.

During 2007 there was a flurry of publicity about a well-known professional athlete who was arrested for promoting dog fighting on his Georgia farm. Pondering the irony of a society that seems to care more about dogs than about children, I searched the reports of the National Center for Missing and Exploited Children (NCMEC) for the same time period as when the dog fighting arrest took place.

During that same week (April 2-8, 2007), the NCMEC received reports of: 2,033 cases in which 1,626 children were used in child pornography; 47 cases of child prostitution; 49 cases of non-family child sexual abuse; 188 cases of children being solicited for sex online; 16 cases of tourism for child sex; 50 reports of children receiving unsolicited pornography through the mail; and 57 reports of children who were tricked into accessing pornography on the Internet.

None of these crimes against children made the front pages of the newspapers that so thoroughly covered dog fighting on a farm in Georgia owned by a famous professional athlete.

When Congress created the National Center for Missing and Exploited Children within the federal Justice Department, one of the tasks assigned to the center was the reporting of crimes against children. In the first fifteen years since these reports were first being collected, an analysis of the crimes against children have demonstrated that in at least 70% of the cases the crime included sexual abuse of the child.

On April 23, 2008, Robert Mueller, Director of the FBI, testified before members of the Judiciary Committee of the House of Representatives that the ability of the pornography industry to use the Internet has increased the volume of pornography, and specifically child pornography, by enormous proportions. In his testimony, Mr. Mueller said, "The FBI has 270 agents working on the Innocent Images program, a multi-agency international operation to fight the spread of child pornography and the sexual exploitation of children online." When asked by a member of the committee to summarize the effect of the Bureau's efforts, he said, "We are losing the war."

The Spread of Pedophilia

Child pornography, or pedophilia, is the graphic depiction of children (primarily under the age of twelve) in sexually explicit poses or conduct. Addiction to pedophilia invariably begins with addiction to mainstream pornography. Why some individuals become obsessed with it is still not understood by any of the experts who attempt to provide therapeutic treatment.

Thousands of case histories demonstrate that eventually a pedophile (the individual addicted to child pornography) so totally loses his capacity to exercise self-restraint that even the certain reality of the loss of family, employment, or personal freedom is not an effective deterrence to his continued indulgence. Pedophiles who "act out" their perverse addiction inflict unspeakable abuses upon innocent, helpless children.

While the creation and distribution of child pornography has existed for generations, it was always limited by geography and practicality until the advent of the Internet. The Internet also has been instrumental in promoting child sex tourism as it readily makes available the location of child-sex facilities and enables pedophiles to make direct contact with procurers who have control over child-sex slaves. In many parts of the world, children are sold or abducted into sexual slavery where they are made available for the carnal satisfaction of paying individuals.

Both our Supreme Court and our entertainment industry have helped to create a culture in which women and children are at risk from predators whose brains have been structurally and functionally altered by consuming pornography (see Chapter 1). For years the pornography element of the motion picture industry has produced films using actresses of a legal age to consent to participate in the production of such a motion picture, but whose facial and physical appearance made them seem much younger.

On many occasions, when an individual accused of raping a child has been arrested, copies of this kind of film were in the possession of the accused and were confiscated by law enforcement officials as evidence of the pre-meditated nature of the crime. However, the pornography industry has continually used its financial and political power to block legislation on local, state, and federal levels that would require the police to determine, in cases involving criminal conduct, if pornography was a factor in the crime. This in spite of the fact that over the past half century numerous law enforcement officers have testified that in up to 80-90% of the crimes that they have investigated involving rape or other sexual assault, pornography was a key factor.

Now that the Internet has brought hard-core pornography within reach of every home, those who want to deal with this issue are falling into the same trap that pornographers successfully baited in the past by opening "adult" bookstores and theaters. Attempting to separate children from adults will do little to solve the problem. When we talk about protecting children from pornography on the Internet, we lose sight of the reality that you cannot protect children from pornography when the adults in their lives still have access to it. We cannot stop child pornography if we do not stop adult pornographers.

Believing we can isolate children from Internet pornography and still allow it to exist for adults is as naive as believing we could insulate children from a contagious pestilence but permit adults to breathe the germs and contaminants freely. Pornography on the Internet is an education system. It teaches. Its message is: human beings are mere animals; the highest value is immediate pleasure; other people may be used and then discarded.

Abusing Children for Money

Since the primary motivation for the production and distribution of pornography is money, the world of child pornography is especially reprehensible. Millions of dollars are spent every month to purchase child pornography by pedophiles throughout the world. The presence in our state prisons of thousands of men who participated as buyers and sellers of child pornography is stark testimony to the addictive power of this most vile form of perversion.

In 1996 the Internet Watch Foundation (IWF) was created in London, England. Individuals around the world provide IWF with reports of Internet sites on which they have found child pornography. In the first six months of 2005, the IWF received and processed reports of 12,000 separate Internet sites containing child pornography, a 34% increase over reports for the first six months of 2004. In the first six months of 2006, the IWF experienced a 35% increase in reports of separate Internet sites of child pornography over the same period in 2005. The current trend continues at this same rate of escalation.

As the IWF categorized each report by confirming the existence of the site and its content, they discovered that:

• There is an apparent growing demand for more severe images, with more than 60% of commercial child abuse websites selling child rape images.

• Eighty percent of the children in abusive images are female and 91% appear to be under twelve years of age.

• Fifty-one percent of the sites appeared to be hosted in the United States.

• Twenty percent of the sites appeared to be hosted in Russia.

• In one 24-hour period, 8,000 hits were counted on one commercial pay per view child pornography site from various countries around the world.

Research with known child sex abusers confirms that adult and child pornography are often used as part of a process to lower a child's resistance and as a means of facilitating the abuse. These reports also show that some sex offenders overcome their own inhibitions by viewing child pornography, suggesting that one of the most critical functions of child pornography is as a reinforcement and justification of the desire to abuse.

Worse yet, almost none of these hideous crimes against children are reported to law enforcement officials. While the actual numbers are impossible to compute, many credible experts estimate that in the United States there are as many as 75,000 children who are forcibly used as sex slaves. Because of our society's overwhelming adulation of sexuality, children today are in greater danger than in any previous generation.

The murder and post-death rape of children who were victims of a pornography addict's unrestrained passion is a repeat of a sadomasochistic fantasy that appears frequently in pornographic materials. Police investigators have reported thousands of actual cases in which a child, teenager, or adult woman has been kidnapped, sexually tortured, and then murdered where a search of the accused's living space has revealed the presence of pornography in which the same crime was detailed.

Every week news items document the increasing volume of pedophilia or child pornography. Arrests for pandering in child pornography have included individuals from University Presidents to otherwise "respectable" housewives. Federal and state law enforcement officials are usually anxious to seek out and prosecute those who produce and distribute child pornography. Yet, many of these officials have abandoned any effort to stem the tide of pornography being produced for adults.

Another assertion – by the ACLU, SIECUS, Planned Parenthood, and others – is that adult pornography is a "victimless" crime. This is tantamount to dancing on the graves of the thousands of child rape victims. The progression into pornography addiction from sexually titillating magazines to the most extreme forms of hard core Internet pornography is well documented. And for every obscene magazine or video purchased, at least two to five individuals read or view it in addition to the original purchaser.

Our Traumatized Youth

Dr. W. Dean Belnap, M.D., a psychiatrist specializing in therapy for adolescents who have become emotionally neurotic because of the sexualization of our society, has given me permission to quote his description of the mental trauma common to many, perhaps most, of today's youth:

> *Let me now take you into the mind of my eleven-year-old patient. She is a victim of anxiety and depression. She doubts her self-worth. She sees no hope that she could ever compete with the glamorized sexualized version of the women on the covers of today's slick magazines. She has difficulty concentrating on her school subjects. She sees no real purpose*

127

in her life and has no vision of a life of fulfillment and happiness. She cannot communicate with any degree of coherence and logic. Her sentences are jumbled, they begin and end with a series of phrases that cannot fit into a rational context. I could go on with other symptoms, but by now you should have the picture.

Dr. Belnap continues:

"Since the year 2008 reports from government agencies have indicated a sharp rise in youth suicide (those less than 20 years old). Commensurate with this trend, statistics indicate an increasing lack of non-verbal communication skills, . . . a decline in academic performance in both high schools and universities, declining social skills and behaviors, and addictive disorders related to sexual imagery. Universities also note a 250% increase in student requests for mental health counseling.

These trends are all frightening, particularly when viewed in light of a previous marked decline in youth suicide between 1993 and 2004. Since 2008 a 20% increase in suicide rates among teenagers has occurred with the number increasing annually. The reason for the increase in these many problem areas has been attributed to a sharp increase in the use of electronic internet/cell phone text messaging and perverse social networking.

The medical literature, especially psychiatric literature, reports a dramatic increase of severe brain dysfunction that interferes with the normal transmission of data through all parts of the brain. All types of addiction among teenagers, including pornography, substance abuse and dependency, sexual imagery and severe eating disorders have increased exponentially.

Among teenagers, text messaging is now dominating much of the day at home, school, church, and during most social activities. . . . Text messaging has surpassed video games as an addictive habit. This increased usage has resulted in Central Nervous System dysfunction. . . . According to reports in the current psychiatric literature, this dysfunction manifests itself in a bizarre pattern of brain mal-functioning that locks information formulation in the left hemisphere of the brain. This information is unable to transfer to the right hemisphere and then up to the frontal lobe for judgment and decision-making.

This gross nervous system failure is the source of a high degree of anxiety that initiates an alarm reaction in the base of the brain where "fight or flight" responses take place. The primitive functions of the basal ganglia of the brain, which are self-preservation, lust, bodily appetite and fear of death, are activated. Such phenomena are the basic causes for addictive controlling behaviors. The documentation of such results has only recently been made possible through the use of modern, sophisticated techniques known as Functional Magnetic Resonance Imagery (fMRI).

This markedly limited brain functioning has serious psycho-social implications including the following:

- Increased mental health problem

- Impaired rational brain mechanisms

- A perverse value placement on sexual imagery

- An increase in the incidence of eating disorders among teen-age girls as they struggle to obtain the appearance of sexualized female idols in the media

- Difficulty developing healthy sexual adjustment in adulthood

• Distorted self-objectification

Our youth reflect our self-indulged culture. Our "feel-good" philosophy of education results in bad behavior, bad choices – and for many teens a succession of very bad days. In search for an escape from the maddening anxiety of a brain gone wrong, today's teens have drugs, alcohol, suicide, sexual indulgence, eating disorders, violence, and the occult. The current data does not just "suggest" that we do something. The facts cry out for parents, educators, and ecclesiastical leaders to give today's youth a sense of self-worth, dignity, and inner peace. If we do not wake up and do something, today's "lost generation" could be the "last" generation. "

(End of the Belnap Quote)

The Truth about our "Decreasing" Crime Rates

During a conversation with the principle pornography investigator for one of the nation's largest police departments, he said to me, "My workload has gone way down. Even though there is more pornography being produced and distributed than ever before, there simply isn't the political will to fight it. When I bring in evidence of a felony violation of the pornography laws on the books, the guilty parties are more likely than not to have the charge reduced to a misdemeanor. They pay a fine and walk out of the courtroom smirking at me. I used to have three other investigators working with me. Now I am the only one left."

In the June 11, 2010 issue of *The Wall Street Journal* there was a guest editorial from a Harvard University professor by the name of Richard J. McNally. The editorial was entitled "Kids Today." The thrust of the editorial was that today children are "safer" than they have ever been. The editorial contained so many mis-statements that I feel it is important to provide the following information. The truth is that our children have never been in greater danger of physical, emotional, and traumatic harm than they are today.

In Aldous Huxley's classic, *Brave New World* (1932), the Administrators created new statistics daily to prove that things were better than before the revolution. The worse society got, the more cheerful the statistics that were needed. McNally's article personifies that strategy. He writes: "Sexual assaults against adolescents have dropped by 67%, aggravated assaults by 74%, and robbery by 72%, while teen pregnancy and suicide are also down."

In fact, any rational examination of the facts reveals just the opposite. The statistics quoted by McNally were based on reports of people over the age of twelve years. The statistics totally ignore the huge number of children under the age of twelve who are the victims of sexual abuse. The FBI National Incident-Based Reporting System (July 2000) estimated that "34% of female sex assault victims" are *under age* 12." The DOJ data excludes rape of children under age 12.

A report from the United States Department of Health and Human Services regarding high risk behavior among persons aged 10 to 24 in the United States during the year 2007 included this statement: "Results from the study showed that 47.8% of U.S. high school students had been sexually active during the year . . . Substantial morbidity and social problems among youth also result from unintended pregnancies and sexually transmitted diseases, including HIV infection . . . 6.9% of U.S. high school students had attempted suicide during 2007."

A homicide expert, former New York City Police Department Lt. Comdr. Vernon Geberth, says today's "sex-related cases . . . are more frequent, vicious and despicable" than anything he experienced in previous decades as a homicide cop.

Less than a week after Professor McNally's commentary appeared, the governments of Canada and Great Britain reported arrests involving a child pornography Internet ring of seven hundred individuals. These individuals were selling hundreds of thousands of sexually explicit pictures of children from just a few months of age up to their early teens.

However, the most stunning aspect of this police operation was that this same Internet ring enabled participants who paid the necessary fee to watch in "real time" the actual rape of a child. Not a videotaped record of the rape; while the participants watched, the child was being sexually assaulted live on camera.

Crimes that are Never Reported

Numerous documented instances confirm that crime statistics are being radically altered in two significant ways. The first is that a number of crimes are simply never reported. According to a 1999 National Crime Victimization Survey, only 28% of all violent sexual assaults are reported to police.

One police officer explained that in their jurisdiction the "way crime was solved was with an eraser." *U.S. News and World Report* (April 24, 2000) discovered the same situation in New York: "Facing political heat to cut crime in the city, investigators in the New York PPD's Sex Crime Unit sat on reports of rapes and other sexual assaults." The FBI found one district "failed to report between 13,000 and 37,000 major crimes" in 2002.

Even more distressing, many other major metropolitan police departments have simply not reported the total number of crimes of record in their jurisdictions. Police Officer Unions from such cities as Denver, Los Angles, and Atlanta have come forward to say that their local police departments have greatly understated the actual

132

number of crimes that investigating officers have reported. This is especially true regarding crimes against children.

Both the FBI and the Bureau of Justice Statistics in the U.S. Department of Justice have consistently estimated that at least one third or more of sexual assault crimes are not even reported by the victim. This is particularly true when the victim is a child.

Also, crimes *committed by against other* children are not always tabulated with those of adults. Offenders are "getting younger and . . . more violent," according to the Associated Press (June 9, 2007). Hundreds of new treatment facilities are being created, for children as "young as 5." AP also reported that juvenile sex predators are being arrested in record numbers. Their review of national statistics on juveniles accused of forcible rape and other sex offenses found an increase of 40% in roughly two decades.

Alaskan lawyer Dennis Maloney calls it an epidemic, with "40% to 80%" of offenders also having been molested victims and "42% . . . exposed to hardcore pornography." Sibling incest offenders, arguably a growing Internet pornography problem, are rarely turned over to police.

Scott Poland, past president of the National Association of School Psychologists agrees, "We're seeing more of it and more sexually aggressive acts. . . . How do these kids even know about this? It's permeated throughout our society."

Credible experts estimate that, in the United States, as many as 75,000 children are forcibly used as sex slaves. Parents who have been encouraged by headlines like "Crime Rate Drops for Third Year Across the U.S" (May 25th, 2010) , should take the time to review the facts. The truth is that because of our society's overwhelming adulation of sexuality, children today are in greater danger than were those who lived in previous generations.

Revising our Definition of Crime

The second way that crime statistics are being changed is that definitions of certain criminal acts have been altered in such a way as to change how offenses are reported. Efforts to "redefine" certain crimes, primarily those involving violence against women and children, began in the mid-1950's. Relying on Kinsey-bred science, some state legislatures across the country were persuaded to adopt a series of statutes that de-criminalized some felonies into misdemeanors and some misdemeanors into "disorderly conduct." As the redefinition became statutory law, local law enforcement officials complied with the revised definition of these crimes. As a result, certain crimes that were actually increasing in number began to be reported in categories of lesser offenses, lowering the numbers in the categories in which they once belonged.

Continuing into the 1960's and 1970's, state legislatures were effectively lobbied to re-define "crimes against the person" and "offenses against morals" as misdemeanor offenses. For example, the original common law concept of "consent" (primarily intended to determine if the crime was rape or fornication) was twisted to move toward legalization of all sexual contacts between "consenting adults." The age of "consent" was significantly reduced in many states - in several states, to twelve years old.

Thus, an accused rapist could more easily use the victim's "consent" as a defense. In some places, forcible rape has become so narrowly defined that the victim is required to prove her resistance by her physical injuries. Many, if not most rape cases, are reduced by "plea bargaining" down to a lesser offense. Thus, according to the official report, that rape never happened. Instead, the lesser offense is the one reported in the annual statistics.

The same way that revisions in criminal law produced the false assumption that crime had decreased (when in fact it had increased), fifty-two sex laws that once protected marriage were weakened, eliminated, or drastically revised through the American Law Institute's "Model Penal Code." For instance, laws regarding divorce, intended to emphasize that marriage as an institution of the state should be protected and enhanced by the state, were changed to grant divorce simply because one partner had "lost interest" in the marriage.

A number of states have dealt with the production and distribution of child pornography in a similar way. In most states, production of pornography is a felony. Since most school children who have cell phones also have photo capability, children as young as ten and eleven have undertaken to produce sexually explicit photographs of themselves or a willing friend. The product is child pornography, and the act of taking the photographs is a felony. Using their cell phones to transmit the photos to others is likewise the felony known as the distribution of child pornography.

In response to pressure from the parents of those children found guilty of these two felonies, prosecutors in many states have petitioned their legislature to lower the offense to a misdemeanor if the perpetrator is less than eighteen years old. In addition to creating the falsehood that there has been a decrease in the felonious production and distribution of child pornography, this redefinition of a crime also denies the victim his or her rights to justice.

To return to a question I raised in my Introduction:
Who is the enemy that has sown the tares? We are! All of us.

We are the ones who tolerated the insulting contempt for our cultural legacy as it was foisted upon us in T.V. sitcoms. We are the ones who left it up to someone else to watch our public schools. We are the ones who never protested as state legislatures overturned and abandoned the standards of decency and dignity that had sustained our cultural morality for centuries.

135

If we are to remove the tares that have been allowed to grow up in our midst, we must return to fundamental principles. It is not too late. The tares have not totally overcome the wheat. We are still able to provide principled leadership in our homes, in our churches, in our communities, in our schools, and in our state and national governments.

If you ask, "What principles?" you can find them plainly set forth in the 20th chapter of the Book of Exodus:

> *Thou shalt have no other gods before me;*
> *Thou shalt not make unto thee any graven image;*
> *Thou shalt not take the name of the Lord thy God in vain;*
> *Remember the Sabbath day, to keep it holy;*
> *Honor thy father and thy mother;*
> *Thou shalt not kill;*
> *Thou shalt not commit adultery (or do anything like unto it);*
> *Thou shalt not steal;*
> *Thou shalt not bear false witness;*
> *Thou shalt not covet they neighbor's house, nor his wife,*
> *not anything that is thy neighbor's.*

These principles facilitated the greatest nation that has ever existed. They can do so again. All that is necessary to make that happen is for its people to make a commitment now.

Chapter Seven

PORNOGRAPHY'S INFLUENCE IN YOUR HOME

During the years that my family lived in California, I had a very close friend named Eric Pridonof. Eric had been born in Moscow, Russia, in the year 1909. On several occasions he shared with me his memories of how his family escaped Russia after the 1917 revolution. His father had been a successful and highly respected electrical engineer, and their family had lived in a very comfortable home in Moscow. One evening his father returned home from work to find the family out in the street. The Bolsheviks had simply come to the door with guns and a mob and had put the family out of their home.

Eric could remember the family's ride across Siberia in a cattle car without heat. He was then a seven-year-old boy. The family owned only what they could hastily grab as the mob ransacked their home. They made their way to the United States only after years of poverty and struggle.

The most poignant part of the story was Eric's memory of his father's agony during the remaining years of his life. Whenever his father would start reminiscing, he would begin to sob and shake his head and murmur, "If only I had listened to those who warned us. If only I had been wise enough to spare my family those years of misery and sorrow. Oh, why was I so blind!" Many are the voices of similar regret regarding the rise of the Nazis in Germany and the incredible toll in human misery and suffering that came from Hitler's insanity.

Warnings that We Must Preserve our Freedom

The loss of respect for dignity, virtue, and the rights of others is the ever-present result of the darkness of pornography. Thus, the protection of our individual rights, both legal and spiritual, requires that we do all in our power to keep ourselves and our loved ones from losing our legacy of freedom and civility. The pornography industry, much of the entertainment industry, and various anti-family zealots are striving to do all in their power to destroy the traditional family as the fundamental political unit of our society. If they succeed, then we will have only ourselves to blame for the consequential loss of our political freedoms.

During the summer and early fall months of 2011, both Great Britain and the United States saw a form of lawlessness that is simply a prelude to what the "alien" generation are ultimately capable of bringing about. In London, New York, Washington, and a variety of other cities in the United States, demonstrations that turned into literal occupation of public and private property were taking place. The demonstrators were seeking to overthrow the established order – the cultural and the economic systems that had been created and protected by law. This gathering of youth had no concern for law nor the rights of property. As this alien generation gets larger and more violent, the extent and the intensity of these demonstrations to overpower the rule of law will increase.

In 2002, Judge Robert Bork gave a talk entitled, "The State of American Culture and What Can Be Done About It." He documented how certain elitists have, in the past fifty years, effectively dismantled the moral heritage and cultural foundation of America. With a truly prophetic warning, he then quoted John Stuart Mill:

> *In all political societies which have had a durable existence there has been some fixed point, something which men agreed to holding sacred . . . But when the questioning of these fundamental principles is the habitual condition of the body politic, the state is virtually in a position of civil war; and can never long remain free from it in act or fact.*

Dr. Bork then commented, "That might have been written about the culture war in America, a culture war in which the judiciary is deeply involved, and for which it must accept a large degree of responsibility. Almost every value, every virtue, every symbol, and every institution once regarded as sacred has now been overthrown or is in question."

He specifically mentioned, the following institutions and symbols: individualism (now radical individualism coming close to nihilism); the meaning of the Constitution as seen by its framers and ratifiers; marriage and the family (now mocked and left unprotected by the courts); the aesthetic environment in which we all must live (movies, music, etc.), now filled with public obscenities and vulgarities; religion (now denigrated and driven from the public square.); and equality, denied by law to some to protect certain racial and gender preferences.

"The first society" wrote John Locke, in his treatise on civil government, "was between man and wife . . ." Fifty years later, Rousseau offered a similar observation when he pointed out that". . . the most ancient of all societies and the only one that is natural is the family." Rousseau continued, "The family then may be called the first model of political societies."

Every significant political philosopher from Moses and Aristotle to Locke, and more recently Arnold Toynbee, have recognized the significance of the family as the basic political unit. It is from the family that any great society, any progressive and growing nation must achieve that degree of stability that allows them to have the internal tranquility necessary in order to progress.

Pornography Threatens our National Survival

Pornography causes the corruption of the traditional family structure and thus the survival of our nation. Almost everyone

139

knows a family that has been victimized because of pornography. The victims wear no bandages, but within the confines of their hearts they are bleeding to death. Almost every family has a pornography victim in their midst although many do not know it. In each story the circumstances differ slightly, but the pattern is the same.

Deceit is the initial symptom. Someone who has become captivated by pornography first deceives themselves with the rationalization that no one will find out; that there is no harm in just looking; that this is the most exciting thing they have ever done. Without realizing it, they have just opened the door to becoming an alien to their spouse, their family, their friends, and their associates at work or school.

As involvement with pornography increases, the changes in behavior move from deception to more aggressive symptoms. Warning signs include anger, withdrawal from association with spouse or family, and lack of interest in the normal routines of life such as school, vocation, and recreation.

Young people of both sexes, when satiated with pornography, abandon all restraint in language and behavior. They become coarse and rude, indifferent to parental admonitions, and unable to discipline themselves in schoolwork or family loyalty. It is as if their persona has been captured and an "alien" brain now has control of their body.

Even in adults, the capacity for self-restraint often erodes away. The greater the degree of perversion in the materials being consumed by the addict, the less capacity for self-discipline they will display. Husbands become abusive of wives and children. Women become contemptuous towards attributes of true femininity that are natural to most nurturing women.

Next comes the devastation of the family's emotional world when the truth is revealed. Whether the victim or the perpetrator is a spouse, a child, a sibling, a relative with frequent access to the family home, or even a trusted friend, the revelation of the truth and of the deception that has taken place, is crushing.

Implicitly or explicitly the question always comes: "How could this have gone on in our own home, our own family, and we did not know about it until now?"

What has gone on is the sexual abuse of a family member, usually a child. In most cases, the computer contains evidence of accessing sexually explicit materials, of secret trysts for sexual purposes, and of the pursuit of bizarre fantasies involving sex. Where children are involved, a cell phone might have texts that reveal an obsession with sex.

Over the years, I have received appeals from individuals and families whose situations have stretched across the spectrum of pornography's power to destroy. The appeal may come from a parent or spouse discovering evidence of pornography in the life of a loved one. I have been a personal witness of the grief and the horror of a family losing a child as the victim of a sex crime alien whose perversion culminated in their child's torture, rape, and murder.

With permission from the authors, I am including here a few first person accounts from my files of the terrible emotional and physical suffering of a wife and mother who discovers that the husband and father in their home is an alien leading a dual life. (Some have been redacted in order to remove accounts of physical abuse in the form of sexual perversions that simply cannot be presented in a document intended for public distribution.)

The Husband That I Never Knew

It was September 1983, and I was on my way to the best four years of my life. I was so excited to be starting my freshman year at the University. School was great, classes challenging, room-mates fun. My life was fantastic. I was studying in the library in early January 1984. I noticed a handsome young man staring at me. He came up, introduced himself, and we began talking. I discovered he had my uncle as one of his professors. We realized we were both from the same area and knew each other's families. The semester went along and we became good friends.

I left to go back home for the summer, and he went to work in another state. The next fall I ran into him again on campus. We had a lab together and began studying in the same group. He asked me out on a date in October and I was so excited. I enjoyed his company. He was extremely friendly, outgoing, and fun. We were already friends, and soon realized that we had something much more. We were engaged. I was so in love and couldn't wait to be with the man of my dreams. We were married in early August that same year. We moved to another state to begin graduate school. We were both in school and enjoying our first year of marriage together.

Then I noticed a change. He never showed affection and was very distant. I questioned him, and he just made up excuses. I was very distraught as this was our first summer together as a married couple. After all, we were still newlyweds! Time went on and things got a little better. At times I felt close to him and other times he was so cold and distant. I couldn't figure out why there seemed to be a wall up that I couldn't break through. I never felt that closeness I longed for in a best friend and eternal partner. I kept trying everything I knew to do to connect with him on a deeper level. We finished school and moved to another state to work. We had a new baby and we were excited to be a growing family.

142

I noticed at that time another change. He was defensive, short-tempered, distant, and cold. I thought it was the pressure of looking for a permanent job. I began to recognize cycles in his personality. He was wonderful at times, and then very cold and distant at other times. This was extremely confusing to me. I began making excuses for his behavior. "He must be stressed," I would tell myself. "He was just raised differently; he doesn't know how to show affection; maybe his family wasn't affectionate."

I didn't give up and was determined to help him with my ability to love unconditionally. We got a job offer the next year. We moved away from all of our friends and family, and it was very difficult. He began working for a firm that was extremely demanding of his time. I was pregnant with our second child and never saw him much.

I began noticing his flirtations with other women. He always spent our date nights looking at any other woman but me. We would be driving in the car and he would look around at women and smile. If I mentioned to him that this hurt me, he would laugh and make me feel insecure. I felt very alone and sad at times. We had our third and fourth children. I continued to be hurt every time we went to a work event, to a movie, shopping, sports event, theme park, church, or any time in public. His deliberate flirtations became more frequent and obvious.

I was awakened in the night and was prompted to go downstairs. He never went to bed with me at night because "he had to work." I crept quietly down the stairs only to find my husband watching and "participating" in a disgusting film. I couldn't believe my eyes! What was I seeing? What was this on our television? I watched for what seemed an hour and he didn't even notice I was there. I finally could not stand it any longer. I became physically ill. I spoke up, and he was startled and became very angry. I started asking him all kinds of questions. With each question he became more angry and defensive. He left.

Once again, I felt so isolated and alone. I prayed that I could forgive him and help him. I loved him so much. I did everything in my power to be a supportive spouse. I felt that I had married him for a reason. I felt I was the one to "save" him. He admitted to me that he had been addicted to pornography since age ten. It all started with viewing pornographic magazines. He had other addictions that came along with that. I knew now why he also had a problem with honesty.

I had discovered more pornography hidden in the trunk of his car. We had been to several counselors at this point, and had spent hundreds of hours in therapy. It was a vicious cycle. We had good months and then several bad months. I was so exhausted. I was tired of meeting with church leaders, counselors, support-groups, etc. just to be disappointed again. I knew in my heart that he would never change. I was promised each time with each new counselor that this was it. He would stop. "This counselor is finally helping me." I had heard it all! I discovered women's phone numbers, dinner receipts, and a post office box key. I discovered cards and receipts from "massage parlors." I discovered a post office box full of pornography and vile movies.

I worked for another five years to save our family. The flirtations continued. The inappropriate names he called other women continued. I found more receipts and proof that his unfaithfulness not only continued, but got much worse. My love for him began to die. It was as if poison was being poured on it each day and it was slowly dying. I struggled for years holding onto a marriage that clearly could not work.

I Was Very Naive about Pornography Addiction

My first experience with finding pornography happened a year after we were married. It was a Sunday, and my husband stayed home from church because he said he wasn't feeling well. I ran across the street to our church and attended the first meeting, then ran home to see how my husband was doing.

As I walked into the apartment, it was dark and quiet. I walked into the hall by our bedroom and on the floor was a pornographic magazine. My heart sank and I felt an awful, dark feeling. I went into the bedroom and asked my husband about the magazine. He told me that a friend had put it in his backpack at school as a joke and he was tempted to look at it.

I was crushed and hurt. I knew I needed to forgive him because he said he was sorry, and I felt he was sincere. Our marriage was important to me and it was very new. I needed to forgive him and trust him again. I did forgive him and soon felt that it was just a one-time mistake and it would never happen again.

A little over a year later, now two years into our marriage, I discovered the awful truth. We had just had our first baby; she was only a few months old. My husband worked nights and would get home around 2:00 a.m. every morning. One night I awoke around 3:00 a.m. and went into the living room. My husband was sitting in front of the television and quickly turned off the VCR. I asked him what he was watching, then walked over to the video machine and ejected the movie. It was a pornographic movie.

I looked at him and asked what was going on. He then admitted to me that he had been addicted to pornography for almost ten years. When he was a twelve-year-old boy he found a stack of pornographic magazines in a field and took them home and stuck them under his bed. That is where his addiction started. As time

145

went on he found himself becoming more and more unable to stop. He tried several times to stop and would go a few weeks or months but then crash and find himself back. Through the years of trying and failing, he lost confidence that he could change. He had struggled ever since.

He only talked to me with honesty about his struggle once I had found out. I was very naive about pornography addiction and had no idea what a destructive addiction it was. I told my husband that he probably needed some counseling, but he said he was too busy at school. I did not know what to do. I did not realize at the time what a terrible and serious addiction this was.

I also did not realize what this kind of addiction could do to a person. I told him that I wanted to help him and that whenever he got the urge to look at pornography, he needed to come and talk to me and I would help him be strong. I also asked for his complete honesty so that I could help. He promised me that he would be honest.

I was just starting to build my trust in him again, when eight months later I discovered what an awful hold this addiction had upon him. My husband had come home from work and was sleeping a few hours before school. I was in the living room with our baby and for some reason I decided to look in his backpack. I opened the front zipper pocket. I couldn't believe it. I had been trying so hard to trust him again and was starting to feel more secure in his honesty. This was shocking, and another painful surprise. I suddenly felt that I really didn't know this person. I called the video store to see what movies were returned last. They were pornographic.

I suddenly felt I had been living with a stranger for two and a half years and had found one lie after another. I confronted my husband and decided I needed to leave him for a week to sort things out. So

146

I took our one-year-old daughter and moved to my parents. The same night that I moved out, I had to go back and get some things. When I walked in our apartment, my husband was sitting on the couch watching a pornographic movie. I then realized what an awful addiction this was. Instead of feeling sorrow that his wife and baby had just left, he felt relief that he didn't have to hide his addiction any more.

Our marriage did not have a happy ending because of the severity of the addiction. He was not willing to get counseling, and I was shown through other powerful experiences that he was incapable of loving. I found out that he had not only lied about his pornography use but he had also been unfaithful, seeing multiple women. I was shown how cold his heart had become because of his addiction. There was not one tear shed when I found out about his infidelity and no sorrow or emotion. He had lost the ability to love or feel.

Since this experience I have done much research and study about pornography and found that pornography destroys the ability to love and replaces it with lust. Lust is short-lived, and the addict will quickly tire of his partner and start looking for someone new and exciting. This is why most addicts usually will have affairs and cannot commit to one person. The sex partner becomes the drug and once that drug wears off, they are looking for someone else. It's not about love at all. It is about lust. The spouse is seen as an object and the addict loses the ability to respect and love his or her partner.

I Could Not Believe this was Happening to Me
The Day My World Turned Upside Down

Called to their home under the ruse of urgently needed babysitting, I was with my three oldest sons, ages 28 to 35. As one held my

147

hand and put his arm around me, another divulged the evidence they'd compiled over several months. Emails from a secret account were put right before my eyes with a cover letter explaining exhibits A through F. My spouse had not only been heavily involved in pornography for at least ten years, but had also been using prostitutes on a regular basis for at least two years – and we now had an inch high stack of documentation of his correspondence with them to prove it.

Thus began the biggest upheaval of my life. Like the millions of others whose marriages and family life have been highjacked by pornography addiction, my life began to unravel. This is my story, but only in the details. The "Porn Addict's Wife" stories are startlingly similar and as common as a cold. The names are changed, but there is no innocence left to protect; all involved end up with dashed hopes, wide-opened-eyes, and broken hearts.

The man I thought I knew has held major leadership positions in our community and is on a respected state board. He's a successful businessman, and made admirable contributions to our family and community. He included nine children in our family business and taught valuable skills to them. He repeatedly emphasized to our children that we should be "building relationships of trust with each other." That irony still carries a sharp sting. Our marriage had lots of challenges to which we both contributed. I had concluded he lacked the ability to mesh lives emotionally with me, but I believed we loved each other and were committed to living according to principles that would keep our family together forever. I was wrong.

Once confronted, with his secret out, he lashed out at one of our sons who told him that his past actions showed he didn't really love me. It became apparent that he truly didn't. I realized that he loved only himself. Yet it had been vital for him to keep me content and in the dark. Our family-life façade was his cover. He had repeatedly told me he had been "happier in the last two years than he'd ever been before in our marriage" because I had "quit trying to change him." I had given up and just accepted things as they were; there didn't seem to be any other choice.

During the two years of our separation, filled with untold frustration, investigation, and trauma, there were all kinds of adjustments. I was on my own. When it became obvious that there was no hope for reconciliation the divorce became final.

People ask me if I'm lonely, to which I reply, 'not nearly as lonely as I was in our marriage.' There is a difference between being alone and being lonely. One can be very lonely in what is meant to be the most intimate of all relationships. I've learned that most people who become addicted to pornography have been users most of their lives.

I have also learned many of the behavioral patterns that are typical of an addicted spouse: secrecy in finances and use of time; social awkwardness, lying, disappearing and going off with no explanation; and the lack of normal desire for marital intimacy. Many of the women that I have met who were married to addicts say they always knew something was wrong in the marriages, but could never figure out what it was. How wonderful to know that I was not the only one that felt that way.

I am not talking about a few rare instances. There is a virtual "refugee camp" of women who have been affected by this "porn plague." They are floundering. They need help. Lives are being shattered by pornography every second, every day – not one at a time, but thousands at a time. It's time that porn producers and distributors be held accountable for the injury and the misery that they have inflicted upon thousands of women and their children. It has to be stopped.

I ran into my future husband at summer camps growing up, so when I saw him in college I knew who he was. He chased me, but I would only agree to be friends. Our friendship of eight months turned into a deep love. We began dating, and I fell in love with his sense of humor and kindness. He cared about me so sincerely and treated me like the most important thing in his life. He was the first boy that I really trusted with my feelings. He showed me more respect than any other boy. I felt safe with him and loved being with him.

At the time, I believed I was the luckiest woman alive. He was a good man. He was my best friend, and we could talk forever. I thought I really knew him. I thought I had covered all the bases of knowing someone before marrying. I thought, "I am safe with him." Most people don't believe my story because it is hard to make sense of what happened to our love.

That day, I knew there was something going on that was deeper than I could have ever imagined. He wouldn't talk to me, kiss me, hug me, or even be intimate with me. He was cold. I didn't know this person. The only things I remember him saying are, "I am leaving," and "Where is the lap top?"

He wouldn't answer any of my questions. He wouldn't accept my longing to hold him and wipe away his tears. While he was packing, I wrote down numbers in his phone that I didn't recognize, hid the laptop, and checked thumb drives. I don't know how I knew to do those things. An angel was guiding me that day, and thank goodness it did because I deserved to know something, anything, of this great shift in my husband.

He, to this day, has not come forward with anything I didn't already find out about on my own. When he drove away, I checked the numbers and the laptop history. There I found the devastating truth of what was going on with him. I called him and asked if he wanted to tell me anything and mentioned that I had found some stuff. His response was, "So what?" About a week after he left, chats with his Internet love popped up. It was horrible.

For the next year and a half, I learned that viewing pornography isn't just looking at naked women. I found videos and pictures my husband had taken of himself, including three different sex profiles. He had been with prostitutes and so much more I won't go into.

I never expected this from the love of my life. All I can say is that it would have been easier finding out from him. I wish he had been honest and given me the respect I deserved by telling me. Instead, over the last year and half, I have been reminded again and again of the filthy life he had been living behind my back.

Pornography changes a person. Seeing how messed up his life is now makes me hurt for him. All I keep thinking is, "Wouldn't it have been easier to just tell me and get help?" Within six weeks of leaving, he got himself into $15,000 dollars of debt. He has spent thousands of dollars on prostitutes; he can't keep a job; and, most devastating of all, he is not there for his daughter. She will feel the pain of not having her daddy around every day of her life.

He looks and sounds terrible. He has told me that he is miserable, but he still won't choose his family over pornography. He is choosing empty fantasies over real love from a human being.

There is hope. It is in the choices we make to stop destroying families. There will be a day when I don't even think about what he did to me. I will move on and detach myself from a husband, but my child asks me questions everyday, like why her daddy is not living with us. Pornography made a selfless, good man into a

151

selfish man. He didn't even think about his child's future. He just thought it was his little secret and what we didn't know wouldn't hurt us.

This is not how it's supposed to be. I am angry that it has hurt my child. And I hurt for my ex-husband's empty future if he continues down this path. Pornography is empty and leaves you alone.

The Dragon

We married on a beautiful summer day, in the right place, surrounded by amazing, supportive family and friends. We had so much potential, so much drive, so much to give the world. We had dreams and goals. I entered the marriage running full speed. I had nothing to fear and no reason to hold back.

I noticed a change in my husband on the honeymoon. He withdrew emotionally. It was as if he threw up a wall where he had been open and free during our dating. I asked him what was wrong. He did not want to talk. He told me he was fine. I did not believe him. The talented, charming, gregarious, caring, helpful man I had come to know and love had become withdrawn, grumpy, short-tempered, and unwilling to work as a team or even help me with the simplest thing. He seemed depressed.

I became pregnant and was extremely sick. I began to feel like something was very wrong. I thought perhaps it was me, something I had done. I searched my heart, wondering what I could have done to make this awful feeling sink into the pit of my stomach.

I left a church meeting early one week in tears. He asked what was wrong. I explained how I felt, and he told me he knew what it was and he would take care of it. He did not include me or fill me in on what was going on. Finally, the therapist told him he needed to confide in me. He told me he had a problem with pornography, but that it was no big deal and that he would repent and we could move on with our lives.

I believed him. I supported him and prayed to be able to forgive. We did our best, but we had no idea what we were dealing with. We had no idea how ravenous the "dragon" could become.

I came home from the store one day and walked into our bedroom. I noticed his notebook open lying on our bed. I normally would not read it. It seemed to me that it was purposefully left and I felt it might give me some answers. I read on only to discover he had written his own "Screwtape Letters," his own struggles with devils, his self-loathing. I cried. I cried for him. I cried for me. I cried for the broken promises and for the damaging effects it would have on our future. A part of me died.

He was relieved that I knew. He told me he was willing to try to get help.

His father passed away shortly after the birth of our second child, and he became severely depressed. I was worried he might be suicidal. We had a loving minister who faithfully looked after him, visited him, spent countless hours encouraging and then sent my husband to counseling.

The counselor had a solid understanding about pornography and how to overcome it. He was very helpful. He met with us individually. He helped me understand that the addiction had nothing to do with me. I had feelings that I was not enough, not enough to fulfill or meet the needs of my husband. The counselor helped me understand I was lacking nothing. He made many suggestions and continued therapy until my husband graduated.

The dragon came for him one last time. He left when I was 8 weeks pregnant with our third child. He had no desire to change. He moved in with his 21-year-old female classmate who had co-published a paper with him. She had no problem with his pornography addition. He came to me and tried to persuade me that if I would view pornography with him then we could have a "normal" marriage. I absolutely refused.

It took me six years to get a somewhat complete story from him about how his addiction started and to what extent was his involvement. I was so worried about the children and how they would handle his absence. It took them two weeks to notice he was gone. That was a huge wake-up call to me. I didn't realize what I had been dealing with every day. When he left, this huge, dark, heavy, awful feeling was gone. I felt peace.

He had taken the dragon with him. He admitted to viewing porn for 20-30 hours a week and having many on-line relationships. He started drinking, but felt it did nothing for him compared to the porn high. He came to me several times wanting to try to make it work. I gave him a list of my expectations, one of which was to break up with the girlfriend. I gave him time to come around. He was unable to meet any of the things on my list. I signed the divorce papers when the baby was 9 months old. I had a clear conscience that I had given it my all. You can never be too forgiving, but you can be too believing. We were married seven years.

. . . .

The common theme in all of these first-hand accounts is the realization that within the outer façade of the porn addict, there was an alien – an alien with whom the spouse could not communicate. An alien who could not express normal tender affection. An alien in whom there were no emotional bonds of love

154

and loyalty for spouse and children. An alien each wife had never really known.

I quote again the statement of the United States Supreme Court in the case of Paris Adult Theater vs. SLAYTON (413 U.S. 49): "There is no conclusive proof of a connection between antisocial behavior and obscene material."

Had one of the justices of the Supreme Court who in their arrogant ignorance wrote the statement from the Paris Adult Theater case that is presented at the beginning of this chapter had a married daughter who had been the victim of the circumstances that are set forth above, that outrageous lie would never have appeared in their decision.

What We Can Do to Heed the Warning

Viewed in a stand-alone collection, the enormous volume and pervasiveness of pornography seems like an overwhelming tidal wave against which there is no hope for survival. We must not be duped into such a myopic view of the challenge to our future survival. There are millions of courageous disciples of Moses and Christ who have the capacity and the commitment to reaffirm the fundamental values upon which our republic was based and by which alone it will survive.

On the entrance to the National Archives in Washington is a quote taken from one of Shakespeare's plays. It reads: *"The past is prologue."* The lesson is obvious and simple. The best way to obtain understanding of the present time is to understand the past. The surest indicator of the future is to look at the present time in the light of the past. The present time will dictate the future, and the attitudes, values, and virtues of the present time will be the most determinative factors influencing the future.

Will the legacy of the present time be the complete saturation of our society by these aliens? If that should happen there will be no need to worry about a future time.

There will not be one.

Chapter 8

"KEEPERS OF THE SPRINGS"

(The following "parable" was originally composed by a former Chaplain to the United States Senate, the Reverend Peter Marshall. It comes from the book, *Mr. Jones, Meet the Master,* Edited by Catherine Marshall, 1950, Fleming H. Revell Company, pp.147 – 149)

"Once upon a time, a certain town grew up at the foot of a mountain range. It was sheltered in the lee of the protecting heights, so that the wind that shuddered at the doors and flung handfuls of sleet against the window panes was a wind whose fury was spent.

High up in the hills, a strange and quiet forest dweller took it upon himself to be the Keeper of the Springs.

He patrolled the hills and wherever he found a spring, he cleaned its brown pool of silt and fallen leaves, of mud and mold and took away from the spring all foreign matter, so that the water which bubbled up through the sand ran down clean and cold and pure.

It leaped sparkling over rocks and dropped joyously in crystal cascades until, swollen by other streams, it became a river of life to the busy town.

Mill wheels were whirled by its rush.
Gardens were refreshed by its waters.
Fountains threw it like diamonds into the air.
Swans sailed on its limpid surface,
And children laughed as they played on its banks and in the sunshine.

But the City Council was a group of hard-headed, hard boiled business men. They scanned the civic budget and found it in the salary for the Keeper of the Springs.

Said the Keeper of the Purse: 'Why should we pay this romantic ranger? We never see him; he is not necessary to our town's work life. If we build a reservoir just above the town we can dispense with his services and save his salary.'

Therefore, the City Council voted to dispense with the unnecessary cost of a Keeper of the Springs, and to build a cement reservoir.

So the Keeper of the Springs no longer visited the brown pools but watched from the heights while they built the reservoir.

When it was finished, it soon filled up with water, to be sure, but the water did not seem to be the same.

It did not seem to be as clean, and a green scum befouled its stagnant surface.

There were constant troubles with the delicate machinery of the mills, for it was often clogged with slime, and the swans found anther home above the town.

As last, an epidemic raged, and the clammy yellow fingers of sickness reached into every home in every street and lane.

The City Council met again. Sorrowfully, it faced the city's plight, and frankly it acknowledged the mistake of the dismissal of the Keeper of the Springs.

They sought him out in his hermit hut high in the hills, and begged him to return to his former joyous labor. Gladly he agreed, and began once more to make his rounds.

It was not long until pure water came lilting down under the tunnels of ferns and mosses and to sparkle in the cleansed reservoir.

Millwheels turned again as of old.
  Stenches disappeared.
   Sickness waned
And convalescent children playing in the sun laughed again because the swans came back.

Do not think me fanciful
  too imaginative
   or too extravagant in my language
when I say that I think of women, and particularly of our mothers, as Keepers of the Springs. The phrase, while poetic, is true and descriptive.

We feel its warmth…
  Its softening influence…
And however forgetful we have been…
  However much we have taken for granted life's precious gifts
we are conscious of wistful memories that surge out of the past –
  the sweet,
   tender,
    poignant fragrances of love.

Nothing that has been said,
  nothing that could be said
   or that ever will be said,
would be eloquent enough, expressive enough, or adequate to make articulate that peculiar emption we feel for our mothers.

So I make my tribute a plea for Keepers of the Springs, who will be faithful to their tasks.

There has never been a time when there was a greater need for Keepers of the Springs, or when there were more polluted springs to be cleansed.

If the home fails the country is doomed. The breakdown of home life and influence will make the breakdown of the nation.

If the Keepers of the Springs desert their posts or are unfaithful to their responsibilities the future of this country is black indeed.

This generation needs Keepers of the Springs who will be courageous enough to cleanse the springs that have been polluted."
(end of quote)

In November of 1968, I met with then California Governor Ronald Reagan in his Sacramento office. I was a member of the California State Senate. I had written a book entitled *We Dare Not Fail* that was an analysis of the failure of public education and government welfare in California. The Governor had read the book and had given it his endorsement as "Must Reading For My Cabinet."

As we talked about what was happening to the family in America, our discussion focused on how certain misguided government programs were weakening the traditional foundation of the family unit as composed of a mother and father working together to provide for and nurture their children. I proposed that Governor Reagan proclaim a week of family prayer dedicated to strengthening the family.

According to California law, such a proclamation could only be issued by the Governor if the legislature enacted a Concurrent Resolution calling upon the Governor to do so. Governor Reagan said, "If you can get the resolution to my desk, I will sign it." Out of that discussion came Senate Concurrent Resolution 45, a copy of which is reproduced herein.

Members of the California Senate were accustomed to my frequent efforts to protect the family unit from the weakening effect caused by the government assuming the traditional role of parents. Many of them resented being forced to make a public commitment in support of these efforts. However, at that time they dared not cast a recorded vote against pro-family initiatives, knowing that at that time the majority of their constituents favored them.

(Photo caption: Governor Ronald Reagan announces his public endorsement of State Senator John Harmer's Senate Concurrent Resolution 45.)

Senate Concurrent Resolution No. 45

RESOLUTION CHAPTER 40

Senate Concurrent Resolution No. 45—Relative to proclaiming the week of February 16–22, 1969, as Week of Family Prayer.

[Filed with Secretary of State February 13, 1969.]

WHEREAS, The home and the family have long been recognized as the most vital factors in assuring a stable society dedicated to principles which will provide for the optimum of freedom, peace, and personal opportunity for growth and development; and

WHEREAS, It is well recognized that within the home, the mother is the most vital influence in building the character and the attitudes of the children who, as the product of the home and the family, become the members of our ever more complex and dynamic society; and

WHEREAS, Recent developments in our country have indicated that a serious downward spiral of moral values is taking place, the net effect of which is to bring to pass a frightening increase in the incidence of crime and violence, a larger percentage of children being born illegitimately, and the very serious increase in the number of marriages being ended in the divorce courts; and

WHEREAS, Now, more than ever before in our nation's history, the preservation of our freedoms, the enhancement of our country's heritage, and the fulfillment of its manifest destiny as a citadel of freedom and the hope of a world torn with fear and strife demand that the American family be sustained in its mission to bring stability and harmony to our society through homes filled with love and dedication to freedom, truth, and the sustaining of the law; now, therefore, be it

Resolved by the Senate of the State of California, the Assembly thereof concurring, That the members request the Governor to proclaim the week of February 16–22, 1969, as a "Week of Family Prayer," dedicated to strengthening the family and particularly honoring the mother in the home to the extent that all families throughout the State of California may rededicate themselves to building a society which will truly represent the finest potentials for human fulfillment that man can achieve; and be it further

Resolved, That a copy of this resolution be transmitted to Governor Reagan.

o

After SCR 45 had been passed by the legislature it was placed on the "consent calendar" on the assumption that it would have no opposition. So I was surprised to learn, the day before the vote was scheduled, that a member of the Senate had asked that SCR 45 be removed from the consent calendar, making it subject to a floor debate and a roll call vote.

I actually welcomed the debate so that I could present to the members of the State Senate the facts regarding the increasing failure of families in California. These facts included the number of children being born out of wedlock, the number of children being supported by public welfare, the huge increases in teenage crime and venereal disease as well as the number of unwed mothers on state welfare and the heart-breaking rise in the incidence of divorce.

When the resolution came up for a vote, we had estimated a debate that would take twenty minutes. It took nearly an hour and a half. Rebutting the arguments raised against the proposed resolution was easy since I had used facts about family failure that had been gathered by the various state agencies responsible for provided welfare aid to individuals and families. The appalling record of public education in the state was also well documented.

At last the real issue of importance to the opponents emerged in the debate. They wanted to change the language regarding what constituted a "family."

Presenting with both subtlety and contrived concern, they suggested that the state should not be expected to position itself on either side of a debate that belonged to ecclesiastical leaders. In February 1969, these apologists for defining a family as "any two persons who wanted to be considered such" did not choose to press their position sufficiently to draw public attention. They knew that the vast majority of people supported the definition of a family as contained in SCR 45.

The resolution was finally adopted by a unanimous vote without any amendments. Governor Reagan immediately issued the proclamation which was distributed widely throughout the state.

Since then much has happened with regard to the legal definition of what constitutes a family. Contempt for the traditional definition of a family as it was defined in SCR 45 has mushroomed into a well-financed and powerful political movement supported by much of the media and all of the entertainment industry.

What You Must Do

This downward spiral and its accompanying desensitization have made the American people unwilling to take whatever steps are necessary to protect and preserve the cultural dignity that is so essential if we are to live as a free people under the rule of law. Our most critical challenge is to overcome the fear that parents have, particularly the mothers who are the "Keepers of The Springs," with regard to opposing the ultra-liberal factions within our society and our public schools that are eroding the foundation of morality and integrity that come from the home.

We must have the courage to speak out for standards and values in public education, the media, and on the Internet that reflect the dignity and virtue that are the historical legacy of the American people. The perversions that are encroaching upon our schools, the business establishments in our communities, and the adulation of sex and violence in our media are creating a generation of aliens . If this trend is allowed to continue the society that we have inherited from our fathers and the political republic so vital to our way of life will be destroyed.

We do not have to be passively tolerant of these perversions. We must give serious attention to the impact upon adolescent minds of the evil that is so skillfully included in what are otherwise supposedly neutral fact situations presented in our schools.

165

Given the reality of what now is, I offer the following proposals for the serious consideration of every "Keeper of The Springs," be they a parent, a teacher, an ecclesiastical leader or a public official.

1. **DEFINE YOUR VALUES.** Define them for yourself and for your loved ones. Values define a family. But what defines the values in a family? One could argue it is those things for which the members of the family spend time or money. The money and the time people spend on items that are discretionary - that is, beyond the basic requirements of food, clothing, and shelter – are those things to which they ascribe the greatest value.

   Purchasing a product or a service that comes from one of the anti-family entities declares support for or acceptance of the values represented by that financial commitment. When children and youth see what their parents choose to do with their time and money, they learn what their parents value.

   You may think that your values are obvious from the way that you live your life. Let me share with you a most powerful personal experience in that regard.

   In my capacity as a California State Senator I became involved in a study of the profiles of youthful offenders in California. At one of the institutions where a group of these youth were incarcerated I had a conversation with a teenage girl who had just been convicted as an accomplice in a gas station robbery that resulted in a murder.

   The reason that I selected this particular girl was because the records showed that the profile of her home and family was so different from that of most of the other juvenile inmates. She came from a presumably stable family where the father was a successful professional. Her mother was active in the community and their church.

As she was brought in for the interview her countenance reflected the agony of soul caused by her situation. Yet I could still discern in her bearing the cultural sophistication of her pre-criminal life.

After we had visited for enough time that she seemed willing to accept my assurance that I was not there to condemn her but to learn from her I posted the essential question. "Can you tell me why you are here? I do not mean the robbery or the influence of wrong friends and behavior. I am looking for some more fundamental explanation as to why you are where you are now?"

After a moment of reflection she gave a very straightforward and remarkably insightful response. "I am here," she said, "because the first time that my parents ever discussed with me what they believed about right and wrong was when they first visited me in prison."

I never met her parents. However, from the comments made by the parole investigator with regard to the home and family I am confident that this revelation was stunning – even shocking to her mother and father. As "Keepers of the Springs" they had no idea of the pollutants that were finding their way into the life of their daughter.

Do not assume that your core values have been implanted in the minds of your children by virtue of what they may see and hear. Specifically define your values and make those definitions tangible and applicable to the lives of your children. It can be as simple as putting up on the kitchen wall a statement of your family values, such as:

- Members of our family are honest in all of their dealings.
- Members of our family understand the meaning of integrity
- Members of our family understand that intimacy in marriage is an expression of love. Sex outside of marriage is an expression of lust and selfishness.
- Members of our family are loyal to our values and loyal to each member of the family.

Parents today have almost no recourse. Laptop computers are required for upper grades at some schools. All communication is done via "drop box" on the computer – no notes sent home. DVDs are pretty much gone. Homework is done by "network" and many DVDs are not available without going to some trouble. Children aren't in front of television so much as on the Internet.

You can stem the tide at your home, but not at your neighbor's. Homework is often on the computer. New movies are part of a series and an adolescent is a cultural misfit when they have not seen the latest "installment." Television shows are sold in "seasons" and a whole season is often watched all in a day/night at a party with friends. Games online present a literal "fantasy" world that your children can enter and stay in all day. School requires so much busywork for so little result that both parents and students alike can hardly stand it. It seems to purposely place parents at odds with their children.

A report printed on December 27, 2008, in the British newspaper, *The London Daily Mail,* warns parents about the dramatic increase in graphic violence being presented in books that are presumably for pre-teenage children. Quoting from the article: "'Vulnerable children, parents and grandparents are increasingly at risk of buying novels without realizing they feature bloody or pornographic scenes,' said Dr. Rona Tuft, a former president of the National Association of Head Teachers. . . . Dr. Tuft's warning follows controversy over two recent high-profile children's book awards in which violence loomed large in the shortlisted novels."

The dilemma for the parent, the religious leader, and the political activist is how to make an understandable lesson for a teenager about the danger of that which, though sexually arousing and titillating, is already an accepted part of our arts and entertainment. We now accept on television, in the motion picture theater, and on the covers of magazines on sale at the local grocery store, images that only a few years ago were considered too vulgar and explicit to be given the right to public display. What was once considered an affront to accepted standards of decency is now totally acceptable in any media.

I have previously quoted from Dr. Victor Cline, Ph.D, a highly regarded clinical psychologist, who authored a book on this issue that was entitled *Where Do You Draw the Line?* For the adolescent generations of the twenty-first century, there is no line. The thousands of images of violent sexual perversion trapped in their brains will make it difficult for them to avoid becoming an alien generation of adults.

PLEASE LET ME REPEAT: DEFINE YOUR VALUES! Define them for yourself and for your loved ones. Values define a family. But what defines the values in a family? One could argue it is those things for which the members of the family spend time or money. The money and the time people spend on items that are discretionary - that is, beyond the basic requirements of food, clothing, and shelter – are those things to which they ascribe the greatest value.

169

2. BE PROACTIVELY INVOLVED IN THE LIVES OF YOUR CHILDREN

One family relations consultant summarized many parental conversations with their teenagers with this example:

Parent: Where are you going?
Teenager: Out
Parent: When will you be back?
Teenager: Later

To accomplish the objective of clear and open conversation with a child the practice and the habit must begin in the earliest formative years. Assuming that your teenager will be comfortable and open in conversation with you is a dangerous assumption unless the habit and practice began before kindergarten and has continued since. However, it is always better to be late than never. Begin now to embrace your children in serious and sincere conversation about their lives and that of your family.

One of the myths that I heard repeatedly from other parents was the assertion that they scheduled "quality time" with their children. For them "quality time" meant that they would set aside an hour or even a day to share themselves with their children in some activity. This hour or several hours or an entire day would come when it was "convenient" to take the time away from the priorities to which they gave greater value than the character development of their own children.

The fatal error in "quality time" scheduling was the fact that their children had friends – a peer group – which whom they were involved every day.

Parents must never forget that the peer group to whom their children have become attached wield enormous pressure in their demands for conformity to the behavioral values of the group. That daily pressure to be accepted as a part of the group becomes an irresistible force in the decision making of its members. Occasional "quality time" is no competition for the loyalty and the acceptance of the peer group.

Have your children bring their friends to your home. It will not take long to be able to detect a potential pollution in the spring of friendship.

Ask for specific details about social studies classes or health education classes at school. All too often exhibitionist teachers will use these pulpits as an opportunity to be contemptuous of such values as dignity, decency, and morality. The springs of public education can be the source of tragic pollutions if the Keepers of the Springs are not constantly on guard.

In my introduction to this book I referenced the fact that my wife and I are the parents of ten children. Thanks primarily to the diligence and faithfulness of their mother as a "Keeper of the Springs," these ten children have blossomed into productive self-confident high achieving adults. Each one of them earned at least two university degrees, and several have three such degrees.

On many occasions we have been asked by our friends to explain how we accomplished this incredible achievement with all ten of the children. So, we asked the children to help us answer the question with a written essay that we could share with others about the formative experiences of their childhood and adolescence.

I cite here just two of the responses that we received. A daughter who distinguished herself academically at one of America's most prestigious private colleges and later earned scholarships to Cambridge University in England and offers for scholarships from four of the most highly regarded law schools in the nation wrote a four page single spaced response to the question. She cited the daily involvement in family prayer, family councils, and family dinners. She cited the "book reports" that their mother required

171

each of the children to write during each week of summer vacation. How often they heard their mother say, "A truly educated person is always learning. There is no summer vacation for your mind." These and other "character building" experiences were constant from pre-school days until going away to a college on the opposite side of the country.

One of her brothers, a physical giant who played football for Navy at Annapolis, and who became a highly decorated Navy helicopter pilot with the rank of Commander, wrote a one sentence response to our request. It said: "Temptation to violate the family values was never a problem for me because I knew that dad would kill me if he ever found out."

Both responses contained the essential elements of our success. Family values were clear and uncompromising. The guidance necessary to understand and never forget those values was an everyday experience.

Please remember my experience with the sixteen year old girl in a California youth detention facility. My purpose in seeking the interview in my capacity as a California State Senator was to learn from her and others what dynamics in our culture would have contributed to their incarceration as a criminal.

> Convicted as an accomplice to the murder of a gas station attendant in a drug related robbery she faced many years in prison. As she was brought in for the interview her countenance reflected the agony of soul caused by her situation. Yet I could still discern in her bearing the cultural sophistication of her pre-criminal life.
>
> After we had visited for enough time that she seemed willing to accept my assurance that I was not there to condemn her but to learn from her I posted the essential question. "Can you tell me why you are here? I do not

mean the robbery or the influence of wrong friends and behavior. I am looking for some more fundamental explanation as to why you are where you are now?"

After a moment of reflection she gave a very straightforward and remarkably insightful response. "I am here," she said, "because the first time that my parents ever discussed with me what they believed about right and wrong was when they first visited me in prison."

There is no such thing as occasional or convenient "quality time" in the formation of the character of a child. That formation requires daily diligence, daily sacrifice, and constant assurance of love and acceptance.

3. BECOME INFORMED OF THE DANGER SIGNALS REGARDING POLLUTIONS.

There are very clear symptoms of pre-addiction involvement with drugs, pornography, sexual promiscuity, video games and alcohol. These things are in the faces of our children everywhere from the magazine stand in the supermarket to the pathetic banal and inane public entertainment.

I am referring to the PG 13, PG 17, and R-rated motion pictures that are patronized so casually. The content of these motion pictures is intended to create an appetite for more graphic and specific sexual conduct. Many of the producers of these motion pictures have as a primary objective the acceptance of adultery, homosexuality, and sexual promiscuity as normal human conduct.

One of the most devastating deprivations for children in the twenty-first century is the lack of any constant training with their father and mother that will teach them the incomparable gift of the value of work. There are numerous excuses for this malady, but in reality the reason that this is happening in the lives of millions of children is because their parents have become so gifted at avoiding the burden of having to teach the ethic of work by example.

In 2005 a reporter for the *Wall Street Journal* by the name of Jeff D. Opdyke wrote an "op-ed" for the Sunday WSJ entitled, *Why Don't Kids Do Chores Anymore?* Mr. Opdyke recited the experiences with his own grandfather in this school of hard work. He wrote:

I don't recall how old I was when my grandfather – who, with my grandmother, raised me- started asking me to cut the grass, though I'm pretty sure I was about 9 or 10. I remember in second grade helping him in the garden and with odds and ends around the house. I also remember hating it: I would much rather have been down the street playing with my friends.

    Looking back, I realize now what my grandfather was trying to teach me then: that you must establish a work ethic; you must learn to take care of your property; you can't always expect money for simply helping the family; you must earn through an honest day's work what you want in this life.

    Many parents – and I concede that I am one of them- are more lenient and less authoritarian than were our parents. When I was a child , my grandparents gave me a chore and they expected me to do it. Period. These days, Mom and Dad aren't so much setting the rules as they are negotiating with their kids. And kids learn to negotiate themselves out of tasks that they do not want to be bothered with at the moment.

    Also, so many kids are over-scheduled these days. They have soccer practice and tennis lessons and dance classes. By the time they get home, there are barely enough hours for homework and dinner. Who has time to weed the garden?

I return to the counsel of my friend and colleague, Dr. Dean Belnap, M. D.

"In the course of my professional career of more than fifty years as an adolescent psychiatrist, I have watched mental and behavioral problems among adolescents more than double. At issue for many is achieving a sense of self-worth, dignity and inner peace. These are safeguards to negative imprinting. A dysfunctional home, absence of a father or mother, or parents spending too little time with their children, are the staging grounds for self-defeating imprints...Self-esteem is a byproduct of wholesome living. It is not the end goal or the end result nor is it the golden road to mental health. Good self-image is a product of truthful appreciation of genuine skills and the sheer pleasure of helping others."

Any committed "Keeper of the Springs" can find volumes of helpful information about the early warning signals of a child or a spouse into whose life some pollution has found its way. All that is necessary is to care enough about the danger of the pollutions to reach out for help. It is there for the asking.

4. FINALLY: SPEAK OUT. DO NOT LEAVE IT TO OTHERS TO KEEP YOUR SPRINGS FREE OF POLLUTION.

In his 2010 presentation to the Lighted Candle Society, Dr. Bryce Christensen, Ph.D., concluded his remarks with this insightful comment:

"Indeed, we must ever remember that what we fight for is more important than what we fight against. That is, we fight against pornography because we are fighting for marriage and the family. We fight for the tenderness and love that we find only in the family. We fight for the patience and forbearance that we find only in the family. We fight for the happiness that we can not only pursue but actually find only in the family. We fight for the natural liberty that grows within the family. So great is family-centered happiness that it is hard not to reach toward

175

another word — let us say 'joy' — as we celebrate the blessing that is the family."

Our founding fathers generally understood that democracy, more than any other form of government, requires self-restraint. They expected that moral education, first in the home, and then from the churches, and then from the schools would inculcate that self-restraint in the citizenry so that the body politic would be governed by law and not by fear of a despotic government.

Their study of history convinced them that the lack of moral values would ultimately lead a people to be controlled by tyrants who could allow the people to indulge themselves in perversions. As Walter Berns has written, "The moral debasement of the sort we are now witnessing never threatens the rule of a tyrant, because his rule does not depend on a citizenry of good character. Anyone can be ruled by a tyrant, and the more debased his subjects are the safer his rule."

Then how does a "Keeper of the Springs" individually participate in the preservation of her children's heritage of political freedom and the legacy of life in a moral society of decency and virtue?

First, she must have a knowledge and how and why government works. Numerous nationwide surveys reveal an abysmal ignorance among our people, especially high school and college students, of our constitutional heritage. She must make a study of how our constitution came to pass and what we must do to preserve it. (The last chapter of this book deals more specifically with this issue.)

Second, she must be possessed of a spirit of sacrifice of time and means in order to fulfill her responsibility. If she waits to participate, to become involved, to do her part until a time when it is convenient, it will never happen. It has never been convenient to earn or preserve liberty, which is so vital in order to have a society of dignity and virtue.

Third, the "Keeper of the Springs" must have the courage to advocate and defend principles of virtue and decency which alone enable a people to be free and self-governing under law. Ridicule of these principles has always been used to destroy the freedom of individuals and nations.

These three virtues, KNOWLEDGE of how and why we are a free people, a spirit of SACRIFICE of time and means to preserve our legacy of decency of self-restraint, and the COURAGE to stand in defense of morality and virtue will enable her, the "Keeper of the Springs," to find the way and the means to protect her home and her loved ones.

Finally, follow the admonition of James in the New Testament: *"But be ye doers of the word, and not hearers only, deceiving your own selves...But whoso looketh upon the perfect law of liberty and continueth therein, (she) being not a forgetful hearer, but a doer of the word, this (woman) shall be blessed in (her) deed."*

The resolution that Governor Reagan signed and published for the people of California still contains the essential factors for the preservation of our heritage of freedom through morality. Any "Keeper of the Springs" anywhere in the nation is free to take that resolution, modify it to suit locale mores, and circulate a petition asking that it be adopted by the various governing bodies, be it the city council, the county government officials, and or the state legislature. The resolution would call upon the chief executive officer elected for that city, county, or the governor of the state to issue such a proclamation.

If enough people rally to the cause the resolutions will result in a proclamation that will give children of all ages a clearer concept of what their parents believe to be right.

There is indeed a secret combination whose mission is to destroy the American Republic by destroying the primacy of the family in the lives of the American people. An essential factor in that secret combination is the international Sex Industrial Complex whose tactics are the use of and the seduction of our youth into the web of pornography.

When a "Keeper of the Springs" finds evidence of pollution in one of the springs that feed her family, whatever that spring may be, she must do more than sit at home and wring her hands in dismay. She must stand up, speak out, and fight for the protection of her family. She must do this because her family is the foundation upon which the Republic is built. If that foundation is allowed to crumble all that we hold dear as a nation of free people will be lost.

Again quoting from Robert Bork:

> *"There is, of course, more to the case of censorship than the need to preserve a viable democracy. We need also to avoid the social devastation wrought by pornography and endless incitements to murder and mayhem. Whatever the effects upon our capacity to govern ourselves, living in a culture that saturates us with pictures of sex and violence is aesthetically ugly, emotionally flattening, and physically dangerous."* (Bork, 1996, pp. 142-143).

How to fight back and the weapons to use in that fight have been set forth by numerous individuals and organizations. There are people in your community, in your own neighborhood, who are already anxiously engaged in that fight. Join with them. Do it now!

Chapter 9
The Survival Of The Republic

We have no government armed with power
capable of contending with human passions
unbridled by morality and religion. . . . Our
Constitution was made only for a moral and
religious people. It is wholly inadequate to
the government of any other.

(John Adams, addressing the military,
October 11, 1798)

Most people who knew me during my political career assumed that my anti-pornography efforts were simply an extension of my religious convictions. To a limited extent that was an accurate assumption, but in fact my primary motivation in fighting against pornography is my political philosophy regarding freedom. Stated succinctly, *I believe very strongly that the greatest threat to our political freedom is the erosion of the strength and the prestige of the traditional family. The most powerful force in destroying the family unit is the loss of moral values.*

To put it in a positive sense, the most vital factor in the preservation of individual political freedom is the people's respect for moral values and their commitment to them. It is the foundation upon which all else rests.

Pornography destroys moral values in the individual, the community, and eventually the entire society. Thus, pornography's ultimate impact upon a society is the destruction of the most essential political unit of that society, the traditional family. No array of nuclear missiles, no legion of armed warriors, no tyrant or dictator, no outlandish political philosophy holds anywhere near the capacity to destroy our nation and our legacy of

179

freedom than that of the insidious spread of pornography among the American people.

Why Should the Government Control Pornography?

When a sufficiently large segment of the population becomes estranged from the virtues and the norms that are the legacy of our nation's founding fathers, we are in danger of losing our constitutional freedoms. The Constitution of the United States was based on the premise that the individual citizens were possessed of those virtues that enabled them to be self-governing under law. Americans have been free of tyrannical despots because they were willing to honor the laws of the land and they were capable of the self-restraint that such freedom under law required. The existence of a common set of moral values thus gave the American people the capacity to be governed under a written constitution.

As a public official I was often accosted with the question, "What concern is it of yours whether or not someone wants to indulge in pornography? That's their own business, not the government's." The most direct answer I have found was given by a British jurist, Lord Patrick Devlin who, as Chairman of a Royal Commission on the issue of pornography in the United Kingdom, wrote:

> *An established morality is as necessary as good government to the welfare of society. Societies disintegrate from within more frequently than they are broken up by external pressures. There is disintegration when no common morality is observed, and history shows that the loosening of moral bonds is often the first stage of disintegration, so that society is justified in taking the same steps to preserve its moral code as it does to preserve its government and other essential institutions. The suppression of vice is as much the law's business as the suppression of subversive activities. (Devlin, emphasis added)*

180

Among the current cadre of revisionist historians in our academies of learning, it is highly popular to denigrate America's founding fathers and to ascribe to them motives and behavior that make their sacrifice in the founding of the Republic nothing more than a self-serving effort for personal economic benefit. Yet all history is searched in vain to find at one time and in one place a more remarkable and brilliant assembly of men. They understood the relationship of moral values to freedom. If they were living with us today, their voices would be raised in continual warning that the result of our downward spiral of moral values will be the loss of our personal and political freedoms.

Their rationale was clear and concise. To be free of tyrannical government, a people must be willing to be governed by the supremacy of law. The greater the commitment to the supremacy of law, the greater the ability to be self-governing under law, and hence the less the need to force any particular pattern of behavior. Edmund Burke wrote of this fundamental political truth:

> *Men are qualified for civil liberty in exact proportion to their disposition to put moral chains upon their own appetites—in proportion as their love of justice is above their rapacity; in proportion as their soundness and sobriety of understanding is above their vanity and presumption; in proportion as they are more disposed to listen to the counsel of the wise and good, in preference to the flattery of knaves. Society cannot exist, unless a controlling power upon the will and appetite is placed somewhere; and the less of it there is within, the more there must be without. It is ordained in the eternal constitution of things, that men of intemperate minds cannot be free. Their passions forge their fetters. (Burke, 1907)*

More recently Walter Berns, in a classic essay defending the justification and need for the use of responsible censorship to protect society from the ultimate result of eroded moral values, has written:

Such was the argument made prior to the twentieth century, when it was generally understood that democracy, more than any other form of government, requires self-restraint, which it would inculcate through moral education and impose on itself through laws, including laws governing the manner of public amusements. It was the tyrant who could usually allow the people to indulge themselves. Indulgence of the sort we are now witnessing did not threaten his rule, because his rule did not depend on a citizenry of good character. Anyone can be ruled by a tyrant, and the more debased his subjects, the safer his rule."

The only way to have a nation whose people can be self-governing under the rule of law is to have people who embrace the moral values that will instill within them the self-discipline to honor and obey the law. In our day we have seen the near failure of democratic self-government in Russia because the people as a whole had no common heritage of morality. Thus the smooth execution of civil and social functions we take for granted could not be achieved in the Russian experience.

Our freedom is totally dependent upon our commitment to moral values. As shown throughout this book, pornography destroys the ability to be self-disciplined through commitment to morality. Thus the spread of pornography is a direct threat to the freedom and liberty that has come to us through our legacy of Judeo-Christian values.

President Woodrow Wilson once said, "Our liberties are safe until the memories and experience of the past are blocked out, and the Mayflower with its band of Pilgrims forgotten; until the public school system has fallen into decay, and the nation into ignorance" (Seldes, p. 604).

The "ignorance" of which Woodrow Wilson spoke is now one of the most critical weaknesses of our social fabric. Our schools no longer teach, as once they did, the vital relationship between moral values and the legacy of freedom that has come to us from the past.

I believe that the acceptance of pornography in our culture constitutes the greatest single threat to our liberty. As the presence of pornography grows, and resistance to it erodes, the essential and fundamental requirements for enduring as a free society are continually undermined and finally destroyed. Our founding fathers knew this, and several of them predicted that if the time should come when the American people would become "corrupted" in their moral values, they would soon lose their freedom.

Robert Bork, whom I have quoted frequently in this book, affirmed this truth as follows:

> It is possible to argue for censorship . . . on the ground that in a republican form of government where the people rule, it is crucial that the character of the citizenry not be debased. By now we should have gotten over the liberal notion that its citizens' characters are none of the business of government. The government ought not try to impose virtue, but it can deter incitements to vice. "Liberals have always taken the position," the late Christopher Lasch wrote, "that democracy can dispense with civic virtue. According to this way of thinking, it is liberal institutions, not the character of citizens, that make democracy work." He cited India and Latin America as proof that formally democratic institutions are not enough for a workable social order, a proof that is disheartening as the conditions in parts of large American cities approach those of [developing nations]. (Bork, 1996, pp. 141–42)

The man who is properly called the father of the Constitution, James Madison, stated, "We base this whole experiment [the Constitution] on man's ability to be governed by law." Madison was reflecting the tremendous influence upon the founding fathers of the philosophy of John Locke, who in his *Treatise on Law and Freedom* wrote:

> *The end of law is not to abolish or restrain but to preserve and enlarge freedom. For in all the states of created beings capable of laws, where there is no law there is no freedom. For liberty is to be free from restraint and violence from others; which cannot be where there is no law; and is not, as we are told, the liberty for every man to do what he lists—for who could be free when every other man's humor might domineer over him?"*

It is said that when the Constitutional Convention was over, a citizen of Philadelphia asked Benjamin Franklin, "Dr. Franklin, what kind of government have you given to us?" to which Franklin responded, "A Republic, if you can keep it."

The citizen then asked, "What do you mean, 'if we can keep it'?"

Answered Franklin, "This Republic will end in despotism, as other forms of government have done before it, when the people become so corrupt that they are incapable of any other form of government." The statements of many others of the founding fathers reinforce and confirm the words of Madison and Franklin.

Our founding fathers also noted that a people could not be governed by law unless they possessed the moral values that would enable them to exercise the self-discipline to obey that law. George Washington, in his Farewell Address, stated:

> *Of all the dispositions and habits which lead to political prosperity, religion and morality are indispensable supports. In vain would that man claim the tribute of patriotism, who should labor to subvert these great pillars of human happiness, these firmest props of the duties of men and citizens. The mere politician, equally with the pious man, ought to respect and*

cherish them. A volume could not trace all their connexions (sic) with private and public felicity. . . . And let us with caution indulge the supposition that morality can be maintained without religion. Whatever may be conceded to the influence of refined education on minds of peculiar structure, reason and experience both forbid us to expect that national morality can prevail to the exclusion of religious principle. . . . It is substantially true that virtue or morality is a necessary spring of popular government.

In his monograph, *"The Secret to America's Strength, The Role of Religion in the Founding Fathers' Constitutional Formula,"* Dr. Cleon Skousen discusses the perceptive analysis of the American legacy of freedom written by Frenchman Alexis de Tocqueville:

De Tocqueville points out that "in France I had almost always seen the spirit of religion and the spirit of freedom marching in opposite directions. But in America I found they were intimately united" (Democracy in America, vol. 1, p. 319). He then points out that the early American colonists "brought with them into the New World a form of Christianity which I cannot describe other than by styling it a democratic and republican religion. This contributed powerfully to the establishment of a republic and a democracy in public affairs; and from the beginning, politics and religion contracted an alliance which has never been dissolved." (Ibid, p. 311).

However, he emphasized the fact that this religious undergirding of the political structure was a common denominator of moral teachings in different denominations and not the political pressure of some national church hierarchy. Said he: "The sects [different denominations] that exist in the United States are innumerable. They all differ in respect to the worship which is due to the Creator, but they agree in respect to the duties which are due *from man to man. Each sect adores the Deity in its own peculiar manner, but all sects preach the same moral law in the name of God."*

185

It was astonishing to de Tocqueville that liberty and religion could be combined in such a balanced structure of harmony and good order. He wrote:

> *The revolutionists of America are obliged to profess an ostensible respect for Christian morality and equity, which does not permit them to violate wantonly the laws that oppose their designs. . . . Thus, while the law permits the Americans to do what they please, religion prevents them from conceiving and forbids them to commit, what is rash or unjust" (Op cit. p. 316). (Skousen, pp. 5–6)*

Lessons about Freedom from History

The French historian, Francois Pierre Giuzot, while visiting the United States, asked James Russell Lowell, "How long will the American Republic endure?" Lowell pondered the question and then answered, "As long as the ideas of the men who founded it continue to be dominant."

The certainty that the "past is prologue" has not been lost on the great teachers of history. Edith Hamilton, in her work *The Greek Way to Western Civilization,* commented:

> *Is it rational that now, when the young people may have to face problems harder than we faced . . . we are giving up the study of how the Greeks and Romans prevailed magnificently in a barbaric world; the study too, of how the triumph ended, how a slackness and softness finally came over them to their ruin? In the end, more than they wanted freedom, they wanted security, a comfortable life, and they lost all—security and comfort and freedom. (E. Hamilton)*

In my youth I preferred reading actual history to novels or adventure mysteries. The ability to read what others had actually done inspired me much more than the fantasies of what people dreamed but never did. In that light I resolved that my life would be committed to doing whatever I could to preserve the legacy and heritage that had come to me through the sacrifice of my fathers. I found a passage in the New Testament that became a personal motto. Written by James the Apostle, it reads: "But he who looks unto the perfect law, the law of liberty, and perseveres, being no hearer that forgets but a doer that acts, he shall be blessed in all his doing" (James 1:25, Revised Standard Version).

This quote at the entrance of our national archives is often repeated but apparently not believed: "Eternal Vigilance Is the Price of Liberty."

In the ancient world there were those who understood the reality that the critical need for "eternal vigilance" was the price to be paid for preserving liberty. One of these was Pericles, who was quoted by Thucydides in his history of the Peloponnesian War as saying: "We do not say that a man who ignores politics is a man who minds his own business. We say that he has no business being here at all."

Ignorance and apathy have ever been the enemies of freedom, the tools by which a legacy of liberty was soon lost. Samuel Adams wrote to his son:

> *The liberties of our country, the freedom of our civil constitution, are worth defending at all hazards; and it is our duty to defend them against all attacks. We have received them as a fair inheritance from our worthy ancestors; they purchased them for us with toil and danger and at the expense of treasure and blood, and transmitted them to us with care and diligence. It will bring an everlasting mark of infamy on the present generation, enlightened as it is, if we should suffer them to be wrested from us by violence without a struggle, or be cheated out of them by the artifices of false and designing men.*

In the battles against the pornographers I often encountered a county prosecutor or law enforcement officer who would say words to this effect: "Yes, I could do more to get rid of pornography in our community, but no one cares. I seldom get a phone call or a letter complaining about the presence of a pornographic motion picture or bookstore. If I had to rely on public awareness and concern to justify my efforts in combatting pornography, we would never make an arrest."

The price of our ignorance and apathy will indeed be a most costly one. Late in the 19th century in Great Britain, Queen Victoria celebrated her diamond jubilee, commemorating sixty-five years of her leadership of the British people. The Pax Britannica that had prevented major war in Europe for almost a century was in full flower. For the great Jubilee, which saw an unmatched gathering of world rulers in London, most British poets and writers penned effusive praise about Britain's might and glory.

Only one saw through the future haze to the reality of what might come to pass unless the lessons of the past were reaffirmed among the British people. That one was Rudyard Kipling, whose somber "Recessional" became a classic prophecy that all too soon was to be fulfilled. In one verse, which seems so applicable to the American nation of today, he wrote as follows:

> Far-called our navies melt away;
> On dune and headland sinks the fire.
> Lo, all our pomp of yesterday
> Is one with Nineveh and Tyre!
>
> Judge of the nations, spare us yet,
> Lest we forget, lest we forget."

By what remarkable arrogance do we presume to defy history's lessons and Almighty God's judgment? By what cowardice or apathy do we turn our backs away from the challenge to our survival—and the duty to arise and meet that challenge?

Author Taylor Caldwell, in her marvelous work on the life of Cicero, *A Pillar of Iron,* attributes to Cicero as a member of the Roman Senate the following prophetic utterance regarding the ultimate destiny of the Roman empire:

> *The daily spectacle of atrocious acts has stifled all feeling of pity in the hearts of men. When every hour we see or hear of an act of dreadful cruelty we lose all feeling of humanity. Crime no longer horrifies us. We smile at the enormities of our youth. We condone passion, when we should understand that the unrestrained emotions of men produce chaos. Once we were a nation of self-control and austerity, and had a reverence for life and justice. This is no longer true. We prefer our politicians, particularly if they swagger with youth and are accomplished jesters and liars. We love entertainment, even in law, even in government. Unless we reform our fate is terrible. (Caldwell, p. 322)*

It would be difficult to give a more accurate description of the peril we now face than was contained in these words attributed to Cicero nearly two thousand years ago. They did not reform, and their fate was in fact terrible.

The Challenge of Standing Up for Morality

A substantial portion of the television industry insists on the right to profit from obscenity, pornography, perversion, and deviancy. Is the pseudo-sophistry of our entertainment industry really going to persuade this nation to accept their "art" as evidence of greatness instead of what it really is – the fruits of inner decay?

Decay begins with the individual and the family, extends to the neighborhood and the community, and ultimately attacks the

189

nation as a whole. Why should we tolerate perversions that are slowly but with certainty destroying the legacy and heritage that gave our nation its birth and sustained its life? Yes, this is a moral issue – one that affects the survival of the Republic.

During the time that I have been actively involved in the fight against pornography, I have been accused of bigotry, pseudo-piety, and seeking to impose my own narrow-minded morality upon the body politic. I expected in this endeavor to be so accused. That was to be accepted as part of the battle.

Those of us who fought pornography have always had to endure the rhetorical tactic: "If you can't refute the message, then attack the messenger." Still, the fact remained that someone had to confront those who market degeneracy to our youth. The commercialization of filth was ever ready to destroy homes and families wherever it could gain an entry into the inner sanctum.

One lesson that I learned early in the political struggle is this: If you believe a principle to be true, and you defend it with knowledge, more often than not those who are contemptuous of your values will not be able to overcome the power of your conviction.

I was once invited to be a guest at a dinner in Washington, D.C., in honor of a close friend who was retiring from a position as a member of the President's Cabinet. During the dinner, I sat at the same table with several individuals who held positions in the higher echelons of the federal government. Several couples at the table had been living together without the formality of marriage or the expectation of any permanency or exclusivity to their sexual partnership. Indeed, for some the current relationship was just one of those necessary stages in their career enhancement among the Washington crowd who traffic in influence with key government figures.

Early in the discussion it became apparent that the majority of the people with whom I dined that evening regarded me as irresponsible, even immoral, because my wife and I were the parents of ten children. Without rancor, I responded that it seemed to me that the total absence of any permanency of commitment, loyalty, or fidelity in the "convenience relationships" of the individuals who openly paraded their current cohabitation represented how much our society had changed in the values that were once deemed the essential fabric of the American Republic. I noted, as a politician, that the essential political unit of the Republic was the family unit, and that those who demeaned the honored status of the family could be regarded as being numbered among the radical militants seeking to overturn the Constitution.

My comments were not intended to be belligerent as much as to make certain that the hearers understood without any doubt what my attitude was toward their contempt for that which traditionally had been the key element to the nation's triumph over challenges of the past.

With regard to my confrontations with the apologists for pornography, I soon found that to be forthright and totally committed to moral values was ever the strongest, most effective weapon that I possessed.

In 1972, on the floor of the California State Senate, I was laughed at derisively by my colleagues when I predicted that if present trends were allowed to continue, we would soon have scenes of graphic sexual conduct being broadcast on television and seen in every motion picture theater around the country.

In a series of televised debates throughout California, I warned that we could not escape the harvest of broken families and ruined lives if we did not enact legislation that would protect the standards of decency in our communities. My opponents in those debates were the same entities noted previously herein, attorneys for the ACLU, the motion picture producers, the magazine publishers, and the television industry.

My predictions of a society being torn apart by an obsession with sexual depravity were always contemptuously depicted as the ranting of a "moral absolutist" who wanted to impose his own values on the rest of society. Yet my worst-case predictions, all of which came true, did not even approach what is now present in our society.

My Final Appeal

My final appeal to my fellow citizens is the suggestion that they unite in the enactment of a constitutional amendment that will restore to the states the authority intended by the founding fathers in the Tenth Amendment, power reserved exclusively to the states and not to the federal government. I suggest that the following wording be used as a model for that constitutional amendment:

> ***Notwithstanding any other provision of this Constitution to the contrary, no branch or agency of the federal government, including the judiciary, shall have the authority to pre-empt or annul by any means the legislative or judicial action by any of the several states which defines, provides for, or prohibits matters or conduct related to the standards of decency or the preservation of public morality within said state or states.***

"We the people" have not been left without the ability to exercise our will. Thanks to the wisdom of the founding fathers, the Constitution contains a clear and precise method for amending it. We the people need only unite in our determination to preserve the moral heritage that created our freedom.

The enticement of pornography has a history of addicting and destroying even the most solidly grounded individuals. Without the protective strength of a home and community truly mobilized against today's obscenities, far too many youth will be enticed into its destructive snare. Once there, they will not only lose the ability to stand faithful and strong in defense of truth and virtue, they will become participants in the great demise of our national heritage.

We must be prepared to wage a continuing battle against any further compromise with the pornographers in our legislatures, Congress, the courts, and the schools. To allow those to succeed who destroy lives in order to gain money and power through the Sex Industrial Complex would be an eternal indictment.

"Your love of liberty - your respect for the laws - your habits of industry –
and your practice of the moral and religious obligations, are the strongest claims to national and individual happiness."

George Washington, letter to the Residents of Boston, October 27, 1789

"It is the manners and spirit of a people which preserve a republic in vigor.
A degeneracy in these is a canker which soon eats to the heart of its laws and constitution."

Thomas Jefferson, *Notes On The State of Virginia,* Query XIX, 1787

Stop being ashamed of what you really believe. For every American, the survival of the American Republic is an essential moral responsibility because the Constitution of the United States is a vital force for freedom and liberty throughout the world. One cannot fulfill the mandate to preserve the Constitution and the institutions of our liberty in ignorance or apathy.

The critical question regarding the future of the American Republic is whether the American people will allow those who produce and distribute pornography to define our culture, our values, and our future. How can a society dominated by sexualized "aliens" survive? Once they are alienated from genuine love and affection, it may become impossible for them to create the basic family structure necessary for the survival of the American Republic.

What are you doing to preserve the liberties and the values that you have inherited from the past? What will be your legacy to future generations?

Bibliography

W. Berns, *"Democracy, Censorship, and the Arts"* (as quoted by
Victor Cline (1974) in *Where Do You Draw The Line?* (Provo:
Brigham Young University Press)).

R. Bork (1996), *Slouching Towards Gommorah* (New York: Regan
  Books).

R. Bork (04/23/2002), *The Wall Street Journal.*

T. Brokow (1998), *The Greatest Generation*, (New York: Random
  House).

E. Burke (1907), *The Works of the Right Honorable Edmund
  Burke,* comp. Humphrey Milford (Oxford: Oxford
  University Press).

T. Caldwell (1965), *A Pillar of Iron* (New York: Doubleday).

B. Christensen (Spring 2010), article entitled "A Capital
  Catastrophe – Why A Little Noted Crisis Portends
  Economic Disaster:, *The Family In America* (Rockford, IL:
  the Howard Center).

R. Christenson (February 11, 1979), "The Judgment of Hustler,
  Sanity, Not Censorship," *Cincinnati Enquirer.*

T. Dalrymple (2005), *Our Culture, What's Left of It* (Chicago: Ivan
  R. Dee, Publisher) (1332 North Halsted Street, Chicago, IL
  60622).

P. Devlin (1968), *The Enforcement of Morals (*Oxford: Oxford
  University Press).

J. Dobson (1989), Transcript of last interview with Ted Bundy,

online at
http://www.pureintimacy.org/piArticles/A000000433.cfm

N. Doidge (2007), "Acquiring Tastes and Loves," *The Brain That Changes Itself: Stories of Personal Triumph from the Frontiers of Brain Science* (New York: James H. Silberman Books), 93-131.

J. L. Fowler, N. D. Volkow, C. A. Kassed, and L. Chang (April 2007), "Imaging the Addicted Human Brain," *Science and Practice Perspectives* (National Institute of Drug Addiction), 4-16.

E. Hamilton (1948), *The Greek Way to Western Civilization* (New York: New American Library).

D. L. Hilton (2009), "It *is* a Drug!" *He Restoreth My Soul* (San Antonio, TX: Forward Press Publishing, LLC), 51-74.

D. L. Hilton (May 2009), "Pornography and the Brain: Understanding the Addiction," Lighted Candle Society Annual Banquet (Salt Lake City, UT), http://ce.byu.edu/cw/womensconference/archive/2011/shari ng_stations/pdf/47b.pdf.

N. van Hoffman (April 13, 1979), "Assault by Film," *Washington Post*, p. D-4.

KETV 7 "From Porn to Prison" (Omaha, NE),

S. Kuhn, et al. (November 15, 2011), "The neural basis of video gaming," *Translational Psychiatry*, 1, e53, dol:10/1038/tp.2011.53, http://www.nature.com/tp/journal/v1/n11/full/tp201153a.ht ml

L. Lederer, ed. (1980), "Erotica and Pornography: A Clear and Present Difference," *Take Back the Night: Women on Pornography* (New York: Morrow).

S. Levenson (1966), *Everything But Money* (New York: Simon & Schuster).

N. M. Malamuth and E. Donnerstein, ed. (1984), "Effects of Massive Exposure to Pornography," *Pornography And Sexual Aggression* (Orlando: Academic Press).

R. M. Perkins (1957), *On Criminal Law* (1st ed.) (Brooklyn, NY: Foundation Press, Inc.).

J. A. Reisman (June 12, 2011), "Journey: A Personal Odyssey to the Truth," http://www.drjudithreisman.com/archives/2011/06/journey.html

J. A. Reisman (1990), *Kinsey, Crimes and Consequences: the indoctrination of a people* (Lafayette, Louisiana: Lochinvar-Huntington House Publishers).

J. A. Reisman (revised January 18, 1993), "*Pornography in Neighborhood Convenience Stores: Neurochemical Effects on Women,*" (prepared for The Ontario Human Rights Commission and published by The Institute for Media Education).

J. A. Reisman (November 18, 2004), "The Science Behind Pornography Addiction," *Hearings before the U.S. Senate Committee on Commerce, Science, and Transportation,* http://commerce.senate.gov/public/index.cfm?p=Hearings&ContentRecord_id=e8088f9f-d8d2-4e82-b012-46337c6f9456&Statement_id=d744db10-1a94-4899-a3ea-fcf5cf0d6493&ContentType_id=14f995b9-dfa5-407a-

9d35-56cc7152a7ed&Group_id=b06c39af-e033-4cba-9221-de668ca1978a&MonthDisplay=11&YearDisplay=2004

A. Salleh (October 16, 2000), "Sex Pheromones Cut Pesticide Use," *ABC Science Online.*

J. Satinover (09 May, 2008), "Jefferey Satinover Statement to Congress on Pornography
http://www.strugglingteens.com/news/RelatedNews/JeffreySatinover.pdf

J. Satinover (May 9, 2008), "Jefferey Satinover Statement to Congress on Pornography,"
http://www.strugglingteens.com/news/RelatedNews/JeffreySatinover.pdf

G. Seldes, ed. (1960), *Great Quotations,* (New York: L. Stuart).

W. C. Skousen, (May 1981), *The Secret to America's Strength,* (The Freeman Institute).

J. B. Smith (2003), "The Twenty Most Popular Videogames Sold In America," unpublished manuscript.

J. M. Twenge (2000), The Age of Anxiety? Birth Cohort Change in Anxiety and Neuroticism, 1952-1993, *Journal of Personality and Social Psychology* (Vol. 79, No. 6) (Cleveland, OH:Case Western Reserve University), 1007-1021.

W. Wagner (February 16, 2005), *Testimony before the U.S. Senate Judiciary Subcommitte on the Constitution.*

F. Wertham (June 1978), "Medicine and Mayhem," *M.D. Magazine*.

D. Zillman and J. Bryant *(1983)*, "Pornography and Callousness," *Journal of Communication*.

(February 2, 1970) *Variety*.

(October/November 2005), *The Religion and Society Report* (Rockford, IL: The Center on Religion & Society).